Enterprise Integration Architecture & Intelligent Platform Engineering

Srikanth Sriramoju
Prashanth Kodati

notionpress.com
INDIA • SINGAPORE • MALAYSIA

ISBN

Paperback 979-8-90392-930-6
Hardcase 979-8-90392-931-3

CONTENTS

PREFACE

Enterprise Integration Architecture & Intelligent Platform Engineering presents a comprehensive understanding of modern enterprise systems and the technologies that enable seamless connectivity across organizations. In today's digital economy, enterprises depend on integrated platforms, scalable architectures, and intelligent technologies to ensure efficient communication between applications, services, and data sources. This book explores the evolution of enterprise integration, architectural patterns, middleware technologies, messaging systems, and intelligent platform development that support resilient and scalable digital ecosystems.

The aim of this book is to bridge the gap between theoretical concepts and practical implementation in enterprise integration. It highlights the role of cloud computing, microservices, artificial intelligence, and data-driven platforms in shaping the future of enterprise technology.

Designed for students, researchers, software engineers, and IT professionals, this book provides conceptual clarity and practical insights into designing integrated enterprise systems. We hope this work serves as a useful resource for understanding and implementing modern integration architectures in a rapidly evolving technological landscape.

Dedication

We dedicate this book to our families, mentors, colleagues, and students who have inspired and supported our journey in the field of technology and innovation.

Their encouragement, patience, and belief in the value of knowledge have been a constant source of motivation throughout the development of this work. We also dedicate this book to aspiring engineers, architects, and technology leaders who are shaping the future of enterprise systems and intelligent platforms.

May this book serve as a small contribution toward their learning and innovation.

ACKNOWLEDGEMENT

The completion of this book would not have been possible without the support and encouragement of many individuals and institutions. We would like to express our sincere gratitude to our colleagues, academic peers, and industry professionals who shared valuable insights and perspectives related to enterprise integration and intelligent platform engineering. Their discussions and feedback greatly contributed to the development of the ideas presented in this book.

We are also thankful to our students whose curiosity and enthusiasm for learning continuously motivated us to explore complex technological concepts and present them in a clear and meaningful manner. Their engagement helped shape the direction and depth of this work.

We extend our heartfelt appreciation to our families for their patience, understanding, and unwavering support during the writing process. Their encouragement made this journey possible.

Finally, we acknowledge the global technology and research community whose innovations and shared knowledge have inspired many concepts discussed in this book.

1

Foundations of Enterprise Integration Architecture

1.1 EVOLUTION OF ENTERPRISE INTEGRATION SYSTEMS

Enterprise Integration Architecture (EIA) has been developed with the development of enterprise computing, digital transformation and distributed business ecosystems. The initial phases of enterprise IT have seen systems built in isolation to facilitate the fulfilment of certain business processes like finance, supply chain, and customer management. These systems were used independently and thus creating fragmented data environments and poor interoperability. The process of integration in this era was mostly manual or even batch based thus causing delays, inconsistencies, and inefficiencies in operations (Gulledge, 2008). The necessity of structured integration architecture was essential as enterprises started growing in order to provide a reliable and well-coordinated system interaction.

The next major change was the introduction of formal methods of data integration. Architectures that were based on batch processing and Extract-Transform-Load (ETL) processes have allowed organizations to unify data across systems, especially to support reporting and analytics. Although it enhanced the quality and reliability of data, it was still mostly unidirectional and schedule-based integration. Connection of systems was made by periodically transferring data as opposed to a constant operational consistency. This phase has prepared the foundation of standardized integration processes although it was not a complete support on real-time business needs (Vallejo, Romero and Molina, 2012).

As systems become more complex and enterprise applications gain popularity, middleware and Service-Oriented Architecture (SOA) became radical models of architecture. Integration was shifted to centralized message layers and service-based communication, with less tight integration between the application. Another feature of Enterprise Service Bus (ESB) architectures was routing, transformation and coordination of services at one common integration platform. This significantly enhanced scalability and reuse, but implementation generally increased complexity to the architecture and governance issues.

The development of cloud computing, APIs and microservices turned the integration around once again. Businesses began to deploy decentralized connectivity architectures that are API based where systems expose standardised interfaces that are to be interacted with. It improved integration to be more modular and scalable and responsive to changing business requirements. Nevertheless, due to the implementation of hybrid and multi-cloud environments by organizations, it became more difficult to ensure uniformity and harmony of operation data between platforms.

Enterprise Integration Architecture is currently being transformed to intelligent, event driven and real time models of synchronization. Contemporary architectures focus on unidirectional flow of data, bidirectional consistency and automated conflict resolution between distributed systems. Integration is no longer a movement: it is the building block, it allows digital platforms, intelligent automation, analytics, and agile operations of the enterprise. This development is indicative of a more general transformation of conventional, batch-based integration to dynamic, smart ecosystems aimed at real-time responsiveness of the enterprise.

1.1.1 Early Batch and File-Based Integration Architecture

Initially, in the history of the development of Enterprise Integration Architecture, there were batch-oriented and file-based models of integration. Enterprise systems in the 70s and 80s were self-sufficient in centralized computer systems. Integration was not intended as a seamless architectural layer, rather, synchronization was made at a specified time period and that was with operational schedules. The technological limitations, lack of network capacity and the lack of distributed computing systems influenced these early forms.

1. **Early Batch Integration Architecture.**

   In early integration, batch processing was the central element. Under this model, data created during the day was summed up and processed as a whole at planned time periods - usually overnight or during non-peak operational periods.

   Key characteristics of batch integration included:

   - Periodic processing of jobs that have been defined.
   - Mainframe based data storage.
   - Large-volume group cycle data reconciliation.
   - Late updates of system based on completion of jobs.

   The batch architecture was suitable in processing large volumes of transactions and financial reconciliation activities. It however brought up latency. Modifications done in one system were not reflected at the other at once resulting in temporary inconsistencies. Real time operational visibility was not utilized in business decisions and instead it was done based on delayed data snapshots.

2. **File-Based Integration Architecture.**

   With the penetration of distributed systems and departmental applications by the enterprises, file-based integration was considered an effective way of exchanging data. Systems would export structured data files, e.g. CSV or fixed-width text format, which were sent to other systems via simple communication protocols.

   The architectural aspects of file-based integration were:

   - Planned production of formatted data files.
   - Transfer through network protocols, e.g. FTP.

- Import and processing in further cycle systems.
- Basic transformation logic in import routines.

File-based integration was asynchronous and schedule-driven even though it was more automated compared to manual methods of transferring. Validation was poorly validated; there was little centralized governance and poor error-handling mechanisms. The architecture relied fully on effective file generation and transfer cycles and was therefore susceptible to partial failures or differences in data.

3. **Architectural Significance**

   The early batch and file-based integration models had a close relationship to operational timing and not business events. They did not have standardized orchestration layers, real time triggers and dynamically routed. This phase notwithstanding, it laid the groundwork of integration principles, viz. formalizing data exchange procedures as well as adding repeatable synchronization mechanisms. These are also structural and latency constraints of this era that led to the emergence of more sophisticated integration model mechanisms like ETL structures, middleware and service-oriented architecture.

1.1.2 ETL-Based Enterprise Data Integration Architecture

ETL is an abbreviation that means Extract, Transform, Load. It is a data integration process that is deployed to bring together data of several sources, transform data and load it into a target system that is either a database or data warehouse. ETL is an important component of data warehousing and business intelligence which enables organizations to make evidence-based decisions.

The ETL paradigm was a significant advancement in how enterprises are integrated and standardized the data movements process into a series of steps and provided specific tools to deal with data pipelines. It assisted organizations to unify operational data in different systems to central repositories to make strategic decisions by reporting and analyzing data.

ETL Process

Extract:

- Data extraction from several source systems, including databases, CRM systems, APIs, or flat files (such as CSV or Excel), is the initial stage.
- By managing data from various formats and sources, the extraction process guarantees that the information is collected in a consistent and useable format.
- Extraction tools include data connectors, web scraping tools, SQL, and APIs.

Purpose: The information from many data sources is obtained during the extract phase. Since the quality of the extracted data directly affects the effectiveness of the entire ETL process, this is the first and most important step.

Etraction Techniques:

- **Full Extraction:** Takes all of the data out of the source. Although it is simple, it may require a lot of resources.
- **Incremental Extraction:** Increases efficiency by only extracting data that has been modified or added since the last extraction.
- **Change Data Capture (CDC):** enables updates in almost real time by tracking and recording changes in the data source.

Transform:

- The convert phase makes the extracted data suitable for analysis by purifying, approving, and transforming it.
- Data cleaning (deleting duplicates, fixing errors), data validation, aggregations, filtering, joining, column splitting, and business rule application are examples of common transformation tasks.
- Because it requires extensive data modification to satisfy business objectives, transformation is the most complicated step.

- Apache Spark, Python (Pandas), SQL, Talend, and AWS Glue are transformation tools.

Goal: During the transformation step, data is processed using various functions and rules to change it into the format needed for analysis. These steps could involve a variety of data manipulation operations.

Common Transformation Tasks:

- **Data cleaning:** Includes eliminating duplicates, addressing missing numbers, and fixing inaccurate data.
- **Data validation:** Verifying that, prior to loading, data complies with predetermined guidelines or criteria.
- **Aggregation:** Data summarisation, such as figuring out total sales by region, is known as aggregation.
- **Filtering:** Using business rules to eliminate data that isn't relevant.
- **Joining/Merging:** Combining information from various sources to create a single, cohesive view is known as joining or merging.
- **Data Enrichment:** Enhancing data by include extra information, like geolocation data or external reference data, is known as data enrichment.
- **Normalisation and Denormalization:** Data organization to remove redundant information or flatten data to make it more accessible.
- **Data mapping:** Involves repackaging data into the schema of choice.

Repackaging data into the appropriate schema is known as data mapping.

Load:

- The last thing to do is to copy the transformed data into the target system which is usually a data warehouse, a database or a data lake.
- The loading process must be performance-oriented and be able to provide consistency and accuracy of data.

- Load operations can be batch-based (loading data at scheduled times) or real-time (continuous data streaming).
- Tools for Loading: Apache Kafka, SQL Server Integration Services (SSIS), Amazon Redshift, Google BigQuery.

Purpose: The load phase involves loading the transformed data into the target system, which could be a data warehouse, database, data lake, or other storage solutions.

Loading Techniques:

- **Full Load:** Putting all of the converted data into the intended location. This method is straightforward, but it has the potential to replace current data.
- **Incremental Load:** Loading just newly created or updated records is known as incremental loading. Among the methods are upsert (update and insert), merge, and append-only
- **Batch Load:** This method works well for huge quantities and involves loading data at predetermined times, like weekly or nightly.
- **Real-Time/Streaming Load:** Loading allows data to be loaded continuously in almost real-time.

ETL Architecture

The infrastructure, data sources, and requirements of the company all influence the ETL architecture. A typical ETL architecture consists of:

- **Data Sources:** Contains a variety of data forms and systems, including online services, flat files, relational databases, NoSQL databases, ERP systems, and more.
- **Staging Area:** After data extraction, it is first loaded into this temporary storage space. Preliminary data transformation and cleansing are done here.
- **ETL Tool:** The main part in charge of the loading, transformation, and extraction procedures. It uses transformation logic and manages data flow.

- **Data Warehouse/Data Lake:** The intended mechanism for loading and storing the converted data. Decision-making, analytics, and reporting can all be done with this data.
- **Metadata Repository:** Holds details about the data, including mappings, transformation rules, definitions, and data lineage.
- **Monitoring and Logging:** Elements for auditing, performance monitoring, error management, and ETL task tracking.

1.1.3 Middleware and Service-Oriented Integration (ESB & SOA)

Middleware is software used to provide communication or connectivity between components or applications in a distributed network, and is essentially software glue that holds different systems together. Middleware makes application development easier and establishes connections between platforms that were not originally designed to connect. Middleware was coined in the late 1960s, when it was usually used to mediate between a client, which is the front end of a program, and a back-end resource, such as a database or mainframe application. In the 1980s, with the emergence of distributed computing, middleware was all the more significant in connecting newer applications with old legacy systems.

Middleware is a platform that enables programmers to create apps without having to integrate with devices, data sources, services, or computer resources each time they need to access them. It facilitates communication via web services, REST, XML, SOAP, JSON, and other common communications formats. Middleware enhances interoperability among systems and programming languages, as well as low tight coupling among systems by offering standardized communication mechanisms.

Enterprise Service Bus (ESB)

"Enterprise Service Bus" (ESB) is an architectural model designed to enable communication between various applications within an enterprise. It uses a bus-like architecture, with information routed between interconnected applications via an intermediate middleware layer. This bus provides a mediator between applications, disconnecting them with one another and making the integration process easier.

The fact that it can transform and standardize the information that is being passed between applications although these applications may follow different data formats or protocols, like CSV, JSON, or XML, is one of the main peculiarities of an ESB. The ESB is used for routing, transforming, and delivering messages to the required service in the required format. The ESB is linked to its services via endpoints which serve as the points of entry and exit of data passing through the bus.

The ESB architecture improves integration logic reusability and flexibility through centralization. Nevertheless, since it represents a centralized hub, it may cause complexity and represent a bottleneck with more interactions between systems.

Service-Oriented Architecture (SOA)

"Service-Oriented Architecture" (SOA) can be described as a software design practice wherein services are loosely coupled, separate, autonomous, and interoperable units of the network accessible software and applications. These services are a feature of business and are capable of interaction with other services across platforms.

Some basic principles implemented in SOA include:

- **Standardized Service Contract:** A service should be described clearly in such way that consuming applications know about the nature of the service and the information it can offer.
- **Loose Coupling:** Services must never be tied to the internal data model or the implementation of other systems.
- **Statelessness:** Services do not suspend data of past transactions and sessions, so do not affect consuming applications to a large degree.
- **Abstraction:** services are black boxes that have no visibility to the business logic of a service.
- **Reusability:** Business applications can be reused across applications.
- **Granularity:** Services are created to be of appropriate size, scope and can be assembled to create composite services.

In practice, middleware, including the Enterprise Service Bus, which provided the structure for publishing and coordinating distributed services, was frequently used to implement SOA. This enabled application interoperability and encouraged modular, reusable integration patterns.

The SOA and ESB implementations however, had large-scale implementations that were complex, and demanded strong governance and generated centralized dependencies. Limits combined with the need to be more scalable and respond to events in real time sparked the evolution in the following generation of integration architectures that are more distributed and event driven.

1.2 INTEGRATION PATTERNS AND ARCHITECTURAL STYLES

The structural background of Enterprise Integration Architecture consists of integration patterns and architectural styles. Whereas integration technologies offer the means to connect the systems, patterns and styles determine the way these connections are to be built. Patterns of integration take a proven solution to an ongoing problem like routing of messages, transformation, error handling, and coordination of system. They are best practices that have been gathered over time and the use of which assists organizations to develop scalable, maintainable, and resilient integration solutions.

Architectural styles provide a more abstract view of the organization of systems and the manner of interaction of parts of an integration landscape. These styles define communication models, e.g. synchronous request response, asynchronous messaging, event-driven interaction or service-based coordination. Enterprises can reduce tight coupling and improve modularity and ensure integration solutions are flexible to changes in both business and technology environments using similar architectural styles.

Over time as the distribution of services and cloud-native services take place, the pattern of integration and architectural styles also transformed as the enterprise systems began to transition to monolithic applications. Messaging schemes, event-based paradigms, publish-subscribe, and service-oriented approaches emerged as responses to the increasing complexity and mass-scale requirements. These models and designs have become the building blocks of the modern middleware and API management solutions as well as in real-time integration systems.

Knowledge of integration patterns and architectural styles is required for the development of intelligent enterprise platforms. They present a systematic approach to integration issues, to be solved methodically rather than ad hoc. The following sections will look at the main patterns and architecture models to explain their role in developing strong, adaptable, and future-oriented integration solutions of enterprises.

1.2.1 Enterprise Integration Patterns (EIPs)

Often referred to as "enterprise application integration" (EAI), "enterprise integration patterns" (EIP) are a collection of principles and practices for optimising system, application, or data integration.

To establish a foundation for configuring integrations without having to start from scratch every time a comparable integration scenario arose, Gregor Hohpe and Bobby Woolf began recording these patterns more than 20 years ago.

Their research has concentrated on characterising message patterns in integrations, or the ways in which integrations transmit and receive data between systems.

When creating enterprise application integrations, which are frequently business-critical and involve a complex ecosystem of data and systems, enterprise integration patterns serve as a crucial foundation. These patterns help business architects design the most effective integrations in situations with many interrelated systems and processes.

List of Enterprise Integration Patterns

Hohpe and Woolf cover 65 distinct enterprise integration patterns in their 2003 book Enterprise Integration Patterns. The majority of the patterns are associated with a messaging situation, in which systems regularly transmit information packets to one another.

To put it more broadly, there are four example scenarios for business integrations, each with its own ideal enterprise integration patterns for configuration. The following are some examples of scenarios:

1. **Data Migration**

   Data is transferred from point A to point B in a data migration scenario. To ensure that data from one location is also available in another, migration can be done regularly or as a one-time event.

2. **Data Synchronization**

   The process of maintaining bidirectional synchronisation between two sets of data is known as data synchronisation. To keep both sets as identical as possible, the bidirectional nature ensures that data flows in both directions. Data may need to be adjusted to match the other application's data model during synchronisation across systems with differing data models.

   One possible solution to the drawbacks of full bidirectional synchronisation is to employ a correlation pattern. Correlation-handling integrations will synchronise only data correlated with the other data set and transfer it only when necessary.

3. **Aggregation**

   Data is aggregated from several sources into a single location in a data aggregation scenario. Although it is acknowledged that not all systems hold the same data, it is still necessary to compile it into a single location.

4. **Broadcasting**

   Data moves in real-time or almost real-time from a single source to several destinations in the broadcasting integration pattern. Every time a transaction or modification is made in the source system, it attempts to propagate that change to all destinations.

Common Enterprise Integration Patterns

- **Point-to-Point Integration:** Enables quick and easy data sharing by directly connecting two systems.
- **Hub-and-Spoke Integration:** By serving as a mediator between many systems, a central hub facilitates scalability and makes adding new endpoints easier.

- **Publish-Subscribe Pattern:** A central broker disseminates updates from a source system to systems that have subscribed.
- **Service-Oriented Integration:** Systems can now communicate with one another through services rather than direct connections thanks to service-oriented integration.
- **Message-Oriented Middleware (MOM):** By holding messages across systems until they are ready for processing, message-oriented middleware, or MOM, facilitates asynchronous data interchange.

1.2.2 Message-Oriented Architectural Styles

The message-oriented architectural style integrates messages and exchanges them via an infrastructure of messages. In place of direct system calls or centralized orchestration layers, communications are processed by intermediary messaging components which are used to process delivery, sequencing and distribution. In this type of architecture, the focus of message producer and message consumers is emphasized and facilitates systems to develop independently but in such a way that communication continuity is not lost.

The use of the messaging mediums like queues and topics to deliver information is one of the principal features of this style. Messages are considered to be self-contained units comprising both payload and metadata enabling routing, filtration and transformation to be done at the messaging layer. Since communication is mediated by messaging infrastructure, systems do not require any knowledge of each other regarding their internal logic, location, or technology stack.

Core Architectural Elements

Message-oriented architectures typically include:

- **Message Producers:** Components that generate and send messages.
- **Messaging Channels:** Logical pathways (queues or topics) that carry messages.
- **Message Brokers:** Infrastructure components responsible for routing, persistence, and delivery management.

- **Message Consumers:** Applications or services that process incoming messages.

These elements collectively provide structured communication control within distributed enterprise environments.

Communication Models

Two primary communication models are commonly implemented:

- **Queue-Based Communication:** The messages will go in a queue where they will be consumed by an existing consumer. The model assists with workload distribution and managed processing.
- **Topic-Based Communication:** Messages are left on a topic and received by a number of subscribers. This model enables the dissemination of information to multiple systems simultaneously.

Architectural Significance

The message-oriented architectural styles have a high level of scalability as the systems can on their own take up workloads. They make reliability through the message persistence mechanism, message control delivery mechanism and distributed processing in multi-technological environment. This style is particularly effective where there is a requirement of high level of availability, fault tolerance and control of data flow within the enterprise ecosystems.

1.2.3 Publish–Subscribe and Event-Driven Architectural Styles

Although synchronous request-response communication-based classical client-server systems were appropriate for simpler applications, they cannot meet the requirements of contemporary information-driven applications. Traditional, tightly coupled solutions like remote procedure calls (RPC) cannot deliver this data fast enough for use cases that demand the fastest possible connection between components.

In contrast to synchronous systems, the publish-subscribe paradigm enables indirect and asynchronous communication, lowering component dependency and enhancing performance by letting each component run at its best rate. Publishers send out "pub-sub" messages, which are packets of data like commands, events, or notifications. In order to get only the communications that are important to them, subscribers indicate their interest in particular channels through which the messages are broadcast.

An anonymous, many-to-many, asynchronous communication paradigm is the publish-subscribe pattern. There are various ways in which producers and subscribers are separated:

- **Space decoupling:** The concept of space decoupling is that neither publishers nor subscribers must be aware of the number of publishers.
- **Time decoupling:** It is not necessary for the publisher and subscriber to be active simultaneously.
- **Synchronization decoupling:** Subscribers can get alerts asynchronously, and publishers can keep creating events without being held up.

Messaging enables high-speed, asynchronous, program-to-program communication with reliable delivery. Programs communicate by sending packets of data, called messages, over channels. Channels are logical pathways that connect programs and convey messages. Each message is a data structure that can represent data, a command, or the description of an event that occurred in the sender.

Event-Driven Architecture (EDA)

Any significant action or state change for a firm, such a customer buying something, a stock price shift, or an inventory update, is considered an event. When businesses are able to record and respond to events as they happen, they become event-driven.

An integration paradigm designed to publish, capture, process, and react to events across distributed systems in real time is known as an event-driven architecture (EDA). All other programs that require notification of an event in one application are immediately notified so they can take appropriate action.

Because event-based architectures are decoupled, apps can communicate data and accomplish tasks without requiring each other to be aware of them. Applications either create or consume events. Producers use a broker to distribute events to consumers in real time. In enterprises with multiple producers and consumers, a broker or a network of brokers is required to enable loose coupling.

Event Transmission and Processing Patterns

In an event-driven architecture, events are transmitted using two primary patterns:

- **Publish/Subscribe:** Attendees of events sign up for the channels and messages that event producers publish. When an event is published, a broker distributes it directly to every subscriber.
- **Event Streaming:** Producers send a broker streams of events. Customers can read pertinent happenings by subscribing to the stream. Even once events are consumed, the broker retains ownership of them.

Once an event reaches a consumer, it can be processed in three ways:

- **Easy event processing**: Customers handle every event as it comes in.
- **Complex event processing:** Customers analyse a sequence of occurrences to look for trends and take appropriate action.
- **Event stream processing:** Using a data streaming platform, users process and respond to a continuous flow of data in real time.

1.3 CORE PRINCIPLES OF INTEGRATION ARCHITECTURE

Significant concepts of integration architecture outline the principles that govern how systems, applications, and services are integrated in a business environment. Although patterns of integration are solutions to repetitive issues, structural approaches are defined in terms of architectural styles, core principles are the design philosophy that ensures integration solutions are scalable, secure, maintainable and aligned to the business objectives. These principles serve as a strategic guideline for making consistent architectural decisions across projects and platforms.

Enterprise landscape is increasing in a distributed format, including on-premises system, cloud systems, SaaS systems, and third-party partner ecosystems, ad hoc integration methods form complexities, redundancy, and operational risk. The architectural concepts are used to prevent fragmentation through imposing uniformity in model of communication, data exchange conventions, model governance and security measures. What they do is to make sure that integration is not practiced as a technical patch but rather as an element of an enterprise strategy.

A clear-cut integration architecture is dedicated to loose coupling, modularity, interoperability, scale and resilience. These principles reduce the dependency of the system, promote the reuse of integration assets and allow the components to evolve autonomously. They also ensure that integration frameworks can be deployed to address real-time as well as operational needs that are batch without affecting reliability or performance.

To sum up, the principles of integration may be considered the key towards sustainable connection of enterprises. They direct the design, implementation, management, and continued improvement of integration solutions so that integration architecture is able to enable digital transformation, smart platforms, and sustainable enterprise agility.

1.3.1 Loose Coupling and Decoupling

The process of linking the elements—also known as components—of a system, network, or software program in a way that minimises their dependence on one another is known as loose coupling. The degree to which one element has direct knowledge of another is referred to as coupling.

Loose coupling decreases the likelihood that a modification to one component—such as a database or user interface—will result in unexpected changes to other components. Reducing the number of connections can make testing, maintenance, and troubleshooting processes easier and help isolate issues when they arise.

The aforementioned components are comparable to specified modules, which provide a simple way to dissect a loosely linked system. Mapping the maximum number of modifications that can be made to those modules without having negative impacts is one method of determining the degree of coupling in a system.

Module additions or deletions, as well as renaming, reconfiguring, rearranging, or other modifications, are examples of such changes. Compared to tightly coupled components, loosely coupled modules are more scalable and interoperable and rely less on other components.

Dependency injections in object-oriented programming give loosely connected software components the resources they require. Dependency injections give the resource code that instructs it on which other resources to communicate with, where to find them, and how to do so.

Decoupling is about making components independent, so they operate as standalone units. This does not mean they do not communicate; rather, it emphasizes that the communication is done in a way that minimizes dependencies, like through well-defined interfaces or protocols.

Imagine Service A processes some data and rather than sending it directly to Service B, it places the data in a common area such as a database or a message queue without worrying about who uses it. Service B, when it needs data, retrieves it from this common area without needing to know which service put it there. By so doing, the modifications in Service A do not have a direct impact on Service B. The services know of a common environment but do not necessarily interact or rely on the other processes of each other.

The final degree of service system independence is decoupling. It provides the greatest level of flexibility where every service can be built, serviced, swapped, or even scaled without affecting the others. This is particularly useful in large, complex systems in which it is necessary to have independence between different components to manage complexity and guarantee robustness.

1.3.2 Standardization and Interoperability

Standardization and interoperability is one of the fundamental concepts of integration architecture that assists different systems, applications and services to communicate, share data and collaborate effectively. Standardization is the process of using data formats, protocols, interfaces and methods of communication accepted by the industry such that systems can interpret and handle common information without having to come up with specialized integration logic each time a connection is made.

Devoid of standardization, every new integration would require custom translation and mapping, which would add complexity to the architecture and the expenses of maintenance over time. Through the definition of shared interface contracts, communication standards and structured data formats organizations can guarantee uniformity between integration efforts and eliminate overlapping development efforts.

Interoperability is the ability that occurs because of the systems be adhering to common standards. The capabilities of two or more systems to share meaningful information and be fruitful with it are the ability. Interoperability incorporates a variety of dimensions:

- **Technical interoperability:** A capability of transmitting and receiving data reliably amongst systems.
- **Syntactic interoperability:** Process of using the structured and agreed format of data, like JSON or XML in order to guarantee that the data is correctly interpreted.
- **Semantic interoperability:** The meaning of data that is transferred between systems is preserved and consistently understood.

The standardization in the enterprise integration context exploiting on-premises and cloud systems as well as external partners can make integration easier and facilitate scalability. When systems follow the standards of the current protocols and data, they can be more easily incorporated into the ecosystem. Standardization facilitates interoperability, which minimizes the amount of errors that are brought about by the incompatibility of formats, enhances automation, and stiffens coordination in diverse enterprise settings.

1.3.3 Scalability and Performance

The ability of a system to provide additional services without seeing a decline in performance is known as scalability. It provides a solution to the fundamental issue of whether the system can be extended to handle additional work. Making sure that systems can grow with the company without sacrificing performance is known as scalability.

Core Scalability Principles:

- **Elasticity:** The ability to dynamically modify resources in response to demand
- **Capacity Planning:** The ability to meet demands for future expansion
- **Resource Scaling:** Increasing processing capacity using a range of scaling techniques
- **Load Distribution:** Distributing workload across available resources in an efficient manner.
- **Architectural Flexibility:** The ability to expand a system without requiring major reorganisation

Scalability Types:

- **Horizontal Scaling (Scale-Out):** To distribute the load, add extra machines or nodes.
- **Vertical Scaling (Scale-Up):** Vertical scaling, also known as scale-up, involves adding more CPU, RAM, and storage to already-existing computers.
- **Diagonal Scaling:** One hybrid approach that combines vertical and horizontal scaling is called "diagonal scaling."

Performance is the speed and efficiency of a system in completing tasks given the prevailing conditions. It gauges the speed, responsiveness, and efficiency of a system in its workload of the specified timeframe. The essence of performance is speed and efficiency it is answering the question How fast can the system perform a task.

Key Performance Characteristics:

- **Response Time:** The sum of time taken to request a full response after placing a request.
- **Throughput:** The number of requests or transactions processed per unit of time.
- **Resource Utilization:** How effectively the system uses CPU, memory, storage, and network resources.

- **Latency:** The delay before processing begins after a request is made.
- **Efficiency:** The ratio of useful work performed to resources consumed.

Performance is typically measured when:

- The system has a manageable number of users and data volume
- Current resource constraints are the primary concern
- User experience optimization is the immediate goal
- Response times need to meet specific SLA requirement.

1.3.4 Security and Compliance

The modernization of the new business landscape presented by the adoption of hybrid cloud environments, Software as a Service (SaaS) applications, mobile platforms, and Internet of Things (IoT) devices has increased the bar of safe integration to new levels. In the face of increased digital presence in organizations, the integration layer has turned out to be a decisive element that bridges differences in systems applications, and source of data. Nevertheless, this integration layer is also an important security and compliance frontier that is seldom appropriately covered within enterprise security strategies.

Such typical weaknesses in security and compliance in integration designs are lack of proper authentication system, lack of access controls, inadequate audit trails, and encryption both in transit and at rest. Unbalances within the organization Business interruptions, issues with data synchronisation, and compliance occur when integration architectures fail breaches that may lead to significant financial and reputational loss in organizations.

The use of APIs has become the most common system of integration in contemporary architectures, yet it has many security threats. Typical attack types are injection attacks in which attackers can abuse API requests by manipulating them to get unauthorized access to resources, authentication vulnerabilities where attackers bypass Inadequate authentication mechanisms and malfunctioning object-level authorisation flaws allow users to manipulate API endpoints and obtain unauthorised resources. The middleware components are easy to integrate, yet vulnerable to message alterations and man-in-the-middle attacks and configuration vulnerabilities that leave sensitive endpoints vulnerable.

Integration architectures have particular requirements regarding the global regulatory environment of data privacy. Within its "General Data Protection Regulation" (GDPR), the data subject rights have been developed, such as the data minimization requirements and the right to erasure. "Health Insurance Portability and Accountability Act" (HIPAA) stipulate security measures to maintain confidentiality, integrity, and access to health information and to provide complete auditing facilities. "Sarbanes-Oxley Act" (SOX) mandates data integrity controls and documentation of movement of financial data in detail whereas the "Payment Card Industry Data Security Standard" (PCI DSS) obliges that payment data be encrypted and that extensive logs and monitoring is done.

Zero Trust model presupposes the presence of both threats within and beyond traditional network boundaries and demands confirmation to any person that is attempting to access resources within the integration ecosystem. This architecture has the continuous authentication and authorization of all integration requests and policy enforcement points, which are distributed across the integration architecture. Strong API security can consist of effective authentication and authorization systems like OAuth 2.0, OpenID connect, and JSON Web Tokens, rate limiting and input validation. "Transport Layer Security" (TLS) and mutual TLS are needed in order to protect data in transit and encryption and good key management practices are needed to protect data at rest.

1.4 DESIGNING AOR SCALABILITY, RESILIENCE, AND INTEROPERABILITY

The present-day enterprises should not just develop an enterprise integration architecture that is aimed at only patching the holes between the systems but also one that is capable of growing, and withstanding failures without collapsing in the multiple technological contexts. As the practice of switching to hybrid cloud systems, distributed services, and API-based ecosystems increases, integration architecture will have to support an increasing workload, irregular traffic concerns, and requirements of cross-platform communication. Scalability, resilience and interoperability is aimed at creating stability, scalability and flexibility of enterprise systems and rendering them to be stable, flexible and capable of further existing.

Scalability is what enables integration architectures to accommodate increasing volumes of data, users and transactions without losing performance. As the digital platforms evolve with the standardization of real-time processing models, then the integration layers must be capable of supporting dynamic assignment of resources and distributed processing models. Without the issue of scalability, the systems are immediately reduced into bottlenecks that limit the agility of the business and efficiency of operations.

The resiliency is implemented to ensure that the integration architectures do not go inactive due to the loss of some components within them. The nature of distributed systems has been vulnerable to network hiccups, service failures and load bursts. Redundancy, failover and fault isolation strategies can be used to eliminate localized failure spread to an enterprise eco system by integration architectures.

The interoperability is a supplement to the scalability and resilience since it enables heterogeneous systems, including on-premise systems, cloud-based system, and third-party system, to communicate properly. New systems fit well in the existing environments due to data formats, clear API contracts and standardized protocols. The structural elements of sound and sustainable enterprise integration architectures are scalability, resiliency and interoperability.

1.4.1 Security and Compliance

Scalability demonstrates a system's capacity to manage increases in workload or prolonged demands without compromising or enhancing performance. Two essential strategies for achieving scalability are horizontal and vertical scaling.

Horizontal Scaling (Scale-Out)

Adding more computers or instances to distribute the workload among a number of employees, machines, or instances is known as horizontal scaling, or scale-out architecture. Load sharing is the process by which the quantity of work is divided among the battery of instances. By increasing the performance of each instance, scaling out enhances the performance of the distributed system as a whole.

For the following reasons, horizontal scaling is frequently chosen:

- **Fault Tolerance:** Horizontal scaling makes use of several concurrently running instances of a program. The other instances can continue to process requests without interruption and offer flawless service even if one fails or a server goes down.
- **Flexibility:** Effective resource use is made possible by demand-based provisioning or de-provisioning. With cloud computing, scaling up or down can be automated based on resource usage metrics.
- **Performance:** Horizontal scaling distributes incoming requests among several instances reduces the load on individual machines and improves overall system performance.
- **Cost Efficiency:** Adding manifold smaller instances to distribute load is often more cost-efficient than increasing the capacity of a single high-end system.
- **Redundancy and High Availability:** Incoming traffic is split across several servers or instances in different locations or availability zones by load balancing. Other instances continue to serve traffic in the event that one goes down, enhancing "Recovery Time Objective" (RTO) and "Recovery Point Objective" (RPO).

Vertical Scaling (Scale-Up)

Another name for vertical scaling is scale-up architecture., involves increasing CPU cores, memory, or storage on an existing system to improve performance. The goal is to enhance the system's capacity to handle higher workloads without changing the overall system architecture.

Vertical scaling is preferred in the following scenarios:

- **Legacy Systems Support:** Some legacy system designs do not efficiently support horizontal scaling, making vertical scaling a practical option.

- **Performance:** Vertical scaling can improve single-threaded performance and increase system capacity.
- **Cost Considerations:** If workload increases gradually and does not require distributed infrastructure, vertical scaling may involve a lower initial investment.
- **Simple:** When scaling up, it is relatively simpler to deploy and maintain as it is compared to managing a distributed environment since it only entails the upgrade of an existing system.
- **Database Scaling:** Vertical scaling An often used database scaling is to add memory, storage or processing capacities to support larger datasets and increased transaction loads.

Finally, scaling up or scaling out is based on the system requirements and attributes and workload. A combination of horizontal and vertical scaling may be adopted to bring balance between scalability, performance, adaptability, resilience and cost effectiveness.

1.4.2 Resilience and Fault Tolerance Mechanisms

Fault tolerance and resiliency are two related terms in the system design, but these two terms are not identical. Although the two are trying to create a reliable and continuity of service delivery, they vary in terms of how they do it, as well as their focus areas. These are two distinct dimensions of which an architect must take into consideration during designing and deploying of a robust highly available application.

Resiliency

The resiliency of a system is the capability of the system to quickly and gracefully recover following a failure or a disruption, even when those failures are not avoided. It dwells on the creation of systems that are capable of recovering, adapting, and fine-tuning down during and after failure. It does not deny failures but allows the system to recover or at minimum carry on with the limited functionality.

A resilient system is one which is able to endure, adjust and recover disruptions or failures and still continue with its fundamental operation. The design of such a system is to not only survive any unforeseen challenges but also be able to recover and carry on with its work within a very short time with minimum losses in terms of performance, reliability, or availability.

A resilient system should have the following features:

- **Fault Tolerance:** Even if some parts fail, the system can still function.
- **Adaptability:** The system is able to adapt to environmental changes, such rising demand or emerging dangers.
- **Recovery Capability:** The system can resume normal operation or acceptable levels of operation that were interrupted in time.
- **Redundancy:** Key essentials are cloned with the view that in case of a failure of any one, the other is to be provided to replace it smoothly.
- **Monitoring and Alerts:** This is through continuous monitoring to identify and act on anomalies before they happen.
- **Scalability:** The flexibility to adjust resource levels in response to shifting needs.
- **Security:** The system is designed to handle cyberattacks and unauthorized access without breaching data integrity or availability.
- **Graceful Degradation:** A partial failure does not result in the complete shutdown of the system.
    - The following are design principles for resilient systems:
    - The replication and redundancy of essential parts.
    - The ability to decompose the system into separate, interchangeable modules.
    - Fail-fast design, which prevents cascade effects by swiftly identifying and isolating errors.
    - An architecture that can grow to accommodate changing loads.
    - Automated alerting systems and ongoing monitoring.

- Frequent testing, such as fault-injection and catastrophe recovery testing.

Fault Tolerance

The ability of a system to function properly even in the event that one or more of its components fail is known as fault tolerance. In order to stop failures from impacting the entire system, fault-tolerant systems are made to identify, isolate, and mitigate them.

The goal of fault tolerance is to use error management, redundancy, and failover techniques to keep failures from affecting system operations. By hiding flaws, it aims to reduce or completely eradicate disturbances.

Among the fundamental ideas of fault tolerance are:

- **Failure Detection:** Systems to determine when a part has malfunctioned.
- **Redundancy:** Systems or backup parts that can take over in the event of a failure.
- **Failover:** When a system or component fails, it automatically switches to a backup.
- **Graceful Degradation:** When a system fails, it lessens functionality instead than shutting down entirely.
- **Recovery Mechanisms:** Procedures that, once a fault is fixed, return everything to normal.

Among the fault tolerance techniques are:

- **Replication:** To guarantee availability, important data or components are duplicated.
- **Error Detection and Correction:** Finding and fixing mistakes in information or procedures.
- **Load balancing:** dividing up the burden among several systems to avoid overtaxing any one of them.
- **Redundant Arrays of Independent Discs (RAID):** To guard against hardware failure, data is stored across several discs.

- **Checkpointing and Rollback:** This involves periodically storing the system's state so that, in the event of a failure, it can roll back to a known good state.

Resilience and fault tolerance together ensure that systems remain reliable, available, and able to recover from disruptions in distributed, highly available integration architectures.

1.4.3 Designing for High Availability and Redundancy

Designing for high availability is critical when building systems that need to function continuously with minimal downtime, even in the face of failures. High availability (HA) aims to reduce the risk of outages and ensure that services are always available to users.

Redundancy

At its core, redundancy involves duplicating components in a system to ensure continuous operation if one component fails. In a highly available system, redundancy can be applied at multiple levels: servers, databases, networks, and storage.

Types of Redundancy

- **Hardware Redundancy:** If a server's hardware fails, redundant servers (physical or virtual) can take over.
- **Data Redundancy:** Data is replicated across multiple databases or storage solutions to ensure availability in case of data corruption or failure in one instance.
- **Network Redundancy:** Duplicate network paths and devices such as routers and switches ensure that even if part of the network fails, traffic can still be routed through alternative paths.

Failover Strategies

Failover is the process where a backup component automatically takes over when the primary component fails. Depending on the system design, failover strategies can be implemented with minimal downtime or without noticeable service interruption.

- **Cold Failover:** Backup components are activated only when the primary component fails. The backup must be started and initialized before taking over.
- **Hot Failover:** The backup component is fully operational and takes over immediately when the primary component fails, resulting in minimal downtime.
- **Warm Failover:** The backup system runs in a reduced capacity and is brought to full operation when the primary fails, balancing cost and recovery time.

High availability architectures integrate redundancy and failover systems to create systems that do not have any single points of failure and can continue to deliver services despite failures or outages of individual components.

1.4.4 Interoperability of Distributed Integration Environments

Data interoperability is variously defined as the capability of the various information systems, applications, and devices to access and exchange, integrate, and cooperatively utilize information across organizational boundaries. It guarantees that the data may circulate freely among systems and with meaning and should not be damaged.

The lack of interoperability results in the data being locked in standalone systems making it less valuable and difficult to respond to the opportunities and challenges facing an organization.

Big Data Principles of Interoperability.

In order to attain a successfully interoperable data, organizations should follow a number of fundamental principles:

- **Standardization:** Use industry standards of data format, protocols, and interface to allow compatibility across systems.
- **Openness:** Turn to open standards and APIs to permit data sharing and avoid vendor lock-in.
- **Metadata management:** Clarify metadata standards to give proper context and allow the discovery of data.

- **Data quality:** This involves adopting strong data governance to achieve data accuracy, completeness, and consistency.
- **Security and privacy:** Secure confidential information via encryption, access rights, and adherence to laws and regulations, such as GDPR.
- **Scalability and flexibility:** Develop interoperable systems that can be scaled to suit the requirements of the business in terms of its scaling to accommodate the growing volumes of data.

Companies are able to establish a strong base of data interoperability by implementing these principles.

Types of Data Interoperability

Data interoperability can be achieved at different levels:

- **Syntactic interoperability:** The capacity to transfer data between systems utilising compatible forms and protocols, such XML or JSON, is known as syntactic interoperability.
- **Semantic interoperability:** Using shared vocabularies, ontologies, and data models, this feature guarantees that the meaning of data is maintained and comprehended uniformly across systems.
- **Organizational interoperability:** The alignment of business procedures, rules, and objectives to facilitate efficient data exchange and cooperation throughout organisations is known as organisational interoperability.

To get the most out of data integration and interchange, organisations must work toward interoperability at all levels.

1.5 MIDDLEWARE, MESSAGING, AND CONNECTIVITY MODELS

Enterprise integration architecture comprises middleware, messaging and connectivity models that form its operating foundation. Whereas architectural principles specify the way systems are to be designed and integration patterns outlines any pattern of common approaches, middleware technologies give the actual mechanisms upon which systems can communicate, share and exchange data, and coordinate processes within distributed environments. Middleware in modern businesses is the connector between the heterogeneous systems, cloud service, databases and applications.

With the increased use of distributed computing, microservices, hybrid cloud environments, and API-based ecosystems within organizations, the connectivity models will have to ensure reliable, secure, and scalable communication. Asynchronous interaction is achieved with the help of messaging systems on the components of the system, which tighten the couple and enhance flexibility. Connectivity organizations dictate the way systems find one another, authenticate, and send data and preserve session or transaction integrity.

There are middle ware solutions, which can be divided into message brokers and enterprise service buses, and API gateways and integration platforms. These technologies abstract the complexity of communication and offer services like routing, transformation, orchestration, monitoring and error handling. Without the middleware, the enterprises would have point-to-point integrations, which would soon become too hard to handle and too big to scale.

The existence of useful middleware and connectivity model ensures interoperability, the resilience and efficiency of functioning of complex digital ecosystems. They offer organised communications that facilitate both synchronous and asynchronous communications as well as ensuring security, governance and performance levels within enterprise integration architectures.

1.5.1 Types of Middleware in Enterprise Integration

Enterprise integration architecture is based on middleware. It facilitates the exchange of information, communication and coordination between distributed applications, services, databases, and platforms. In enterprise-level systems, middleware decouples the complexity of heterogeneous systems and offers standardized routing, transformation, transaction management, and delivery of messages.

In the sphere of enterprise integration, the most relevant categories of middleware are the following ones:

1. **Application Programming Interface (API) Middleware:** API middleware is a middleware that enables tools and infrastructure with which application interfaces can be created, managed, and exposed. It can facilitate systems communication based on service contracts and facilitates request routing, protocol mediation, enforcement of authentication, and traffic control. Middleware API is a core element in supporting services based and microservices based architecture in contemporary businesses.

2. **Application Server Middleware:** Application servers make a controlled run-time platform to enterprise applications. They provide basic services like security management, coordination of transactions, session control, resource pooling and concurrency management. Application servers provide scalable multi-tier designs by concentrating these capabilities and provide the execution of the business logic in a consistent way across the distributed systems.

3. **Application Integration Middleware (EAI):** Enterprise Application Integration (EAI) middleware facilitates communication between the heterogeneous enterprise systems. It is used to route, transform, orchestrate and mediate messages across business applications. Instead of using direct point to point connections, EAI middle ware offers a structured integration layer that eases the interconnectivity of systems and makes systems architectures simpler.

4. **Data Integration Middleware:** Data integration middleware aims at providing a consistent access, transformation, and synchronization of data between systems. It aids in interchange of structured data, schema mapping and mediation of data across platforms. This category is used to make sure that enterprise data can be shared and consumed in a reliable way without affecting integrity or consistency.

5. **Message-Oriented Middleware (MOM):** Message-Oriented Middleware allows the asynchronous messages between distributed components using queues of messages or brokers. It deals with routing of messages, reliable delivery, ordering and persistence. MOM increases the scalability, flexibility and fault isolation in enterprise integration setting by decoupling between senders and receivers.

6. **Remote Procedure Call (RPC) Middleware:** RPC middleware is a type of middleware that enables one application to call a procedure or a service on a different system over a network. It supports distributed communication which is similar to local procedure calls. RPC-based connectivity is more friendly to synchronous interaction and is frequently employed in situations where the immediate response is needed and that the operations are more or less coordinated.

7. **Object Request Broker (ORB):** Object Request Broker middleware has the benefit of communicating between distributed objects without the knowledge of their physical location or internal implementation. It allows cross system interoperability, by abstracting the interactions of objects in distributed systems.

8. **Transaction Processing (TP) Middleware:** Transaction processing middleware is used to facilitate coordinated completion of distributed transactions among several systems. It provides consistency, atomicity and reliability of inter-resource operations. This is necessary in business settings that deal with financial, operational or mission-critical loads.

All these middleware types provide the structural mechanisms of connectivity, messaging, coordination and distributed processing of enterprise integration architectures. With appropriate selection of middleware paradigms, organizations are able to derive integration structures, which are scalable, robust and interoperable among digital ecosystems with complexities.

1.5.2 Messaging Infrastructure and Delivery Mechanisms

The enterprise integration messaging system uses its fundamental protocol to create a dependable system that delivers secure information through an ordered process between its multiple remote systems. Business messaging systems deliver operators with delivery control and buffering and retry capabilities and route functions which separate communication processing from application function.

1. **Message Structure**

   A message typically consists of:

   - **Header** – Contains metadata about the sender and the destination and the timestamp and the routing details and the security credentials.
   - **Body (Payload)** – Contains the actual business data being transmitted.

   The system allows separate handling of header and payload which enables different routing methods and policy enforcement without changing business data.

2. **Delivery** Guarantees

   Enterprise messaging systems support different delivery semantics:

   - **At-most-once delivery** – Message is delivered once or not at all.
   - **At-least-once delivery** – Message may be delivered more than once but is guaranteed to be delivered.
   - **Exactly-once delivery** – Message is delivered only once without duplication.

   These guarantees are critical in financial, transactional, and mission-critical systems.

3. **Message Routing**

   Messaging middleware supports:

- Content-based routing
- Rule-based routing
- Channel-based routing

Routing logic determines how messages are directed to appropriate consumers.

Message Persistence and Durability

Messaging systems used in an enterprise usually archive messages to avoid loss upon failure. Persistent messaging brings about a situation whereby messages are not lost in case consumers are unavailable at that time.

Broker-Based Messaging

Modern architectures use message brokers to:

- Decouple producers and consumers
- Manage message queues and topics
- Handle load balancing
- Provide monitoring and logging

1.5.3 Types of Middleware in Enterprise Integration

Connectivity models in enterprise integration architectures define the interactions and information exchange between the distributed systems' environments. The decision about whether to use synchronous or asynchronous communication has a major influence on system responsiveness, scalability, fault tolerance, and operational flexibility. These models dictate the behavior of awaiting the response of a system or proceeds on its own after initiating communication.

1. **Synchronous Communication**

   In a synchronous communication, a system will send request to another system and await the response before proceeding with execution. The requesting part is held until the response is received or a time out has taken place.

   This model is commonly used in:

- REST API interactions
- SQL database queries
- Remote Procedure Calls (RPC)
- Real-time service validations

Characteristics

- Immediate request–response interaction
- Temporal dependency between communicating systems
- Blocking behavior during processing
- Strong coupling between client and service

Advantages

- Predictable control flow
- Simplified transaction management
- Easier error detection and handling
- Suitable for real-time operations requiring instant confirmation

Disadvantages

- Increased latency due to blocking
- Reduced scalability under heavy load
- Higher sensitivity to network failures
- Potential cascading failures in tightly coupled systems

Synchronous communication is especially suitable when there is a need to determine validity or confirmation that needs to be made immediate within an operation that includes authentication, payment authorization as well as verification of transactional data.

2. **Asynchronous Communication**

In an asynchronous communication a message is sent off by the system without expecting the receiver to respond instantly. The message is normally sent via additional element like a message queue or broker. The message is processed by the receiving system and can give a later reaction when necessary.

This model is widely used in:

- Message queue systems (e.g., RabbitMQ, Kafka, AWS SQS)
- Event-driven workflows
- Background job processing
- Large-scale data streaming environments

Characteristics

- Non-blocking communication
- Temporal independence between sender and receiver
- Decoupled service interaction
- Improved resilience to temporary failures

Advantages

- Enhanced scalability
- Better fault tolerance
- Reduced service dependencies
- Efficient handling of high-volume workloads

Disadvantages

- More complex error handling
- Increased difficulty in monitoring and debugging
- Challenges in maintaining strict data consistency

Asynchronous communication would be especially efficient in distributed systems where scalability, resiliency, and workload distribution are vital design factors.

3. **Hybrid Connectivity Approaches**

Contemporary enterprise systems usually integrate both synchronous and asynchronous communication. Synchronous interaction may be used for critical operations that require immediate confirmation, whereas non-critical, long-running processes that demand high volume may be handled asynchronously via messaging.

A hybrid implementation allows organizations to trade off performance, reliability, scalability, and responsiveness in complex integration architectures.

By appropriately selecting and integrating connectivity models, enterprise architects can design integration architectures that enable continuity of operations, effective resource use, and resilient system behavior across dispersed environments.

Multiple Choice Questions (MCQs)

1. **Which of the following was the earliest method used for enterprise system integration?**

   A. Service-Oriented Architecture (SOA)

   B. Microservices Architecture

   C. Point-to-Point Integration

   D. API Gateway

2. **Enterprise Application Integration (EAI) was primarily introduced to:**

   A. Replace databases

   B. Reduce complexity of multiple point-to-point connections

   C. Eliminate middleware

   D. Increase hardware performance

3. **Which architectural style allows independent services to communicate through standardized interfaces?**

   A. Monolithic Architecture

   B. Service-Oriented Architecture (SOA)

   C. Standalone Architecture

   D. Batch Processing Architecture

4. **In an Event-Driven Architecture, communication between systems occurs through:**

   A. Direct database sharing

   B. File transfer

   C. Events and message brokers

   D. Manual synchronization

5. **Which principle ensures that different systems can exchange and use information effectively?**

   A. Scalability

   B. Interoperability

   C. Redundancy

   D. Isolation

6. **Loose coupling in integration architecture means:**

   A. Systems are tightly dependent on each other

   B. Systems communicate through shared databases

   C. Systems interact with minimal dependency

   D. Systems are merged into a single application

7. **Scalability in integration architecture refers to:**
   A. Reducing the number of users
   B. Increasing system capacity to handle growing workloads
   C. Limiting application access
   D. Removing integration layers
8. **Which mechanism improves system resilience by allowing recovery from failures?**
   A. Load balancing
   B. Fault tolerance and redundancy
   C. Data compression
   D. Static routing
9. **Middleware in enterprise integration primarily acts as:**
   A. A hardware device for storage
   B. A layer that enables communication between applications
   C. A replacement for operating systems
   D. A user interface tool
10. **Which messaging model allows asynchronous communication between systems?**
   A. Request–Response Model
   B. Publish–Subscribe Model
   C. Direct Database Access
   D. Manual Data Entry

Answers

1	2	3	4	5	6	7	8	9	10
C	B	B	C	B	C	B	B	B	B

2

API-First and Event-Driven Integration Platforms

2.1 API-FIRST STRATEGY AND CONTRACT-DRIVEN DESIGN

Enterprise AI has entered its current stage of development. Automated systems used in the past operated through scheduled operations which followed specific tasks. The agentic AI now handles all work through its process of understanding and selecting actions. The systems possess the ability to comprehend their surroundings, handle different situations, collaborate with others, and perform important activities in complicated operational settings. The transition represents a complete transformation of how technology supported IT teams in their operations. AI serves as an additional stakeholder which helps organizations manage their operational speed and system interruptions while maintaining operational capacity.

The enterprise integration architecture experiences direct effects from this transformation. The systems are not created to be predictable in processing requests and responses, but to facilitate interaction between the intelligent agents, services and humans continuously. Layers of integration are now required to support contextual interactions, long-running processes and orchestration (Xu, 2014)a scientific and engineering discipline called Industrial Information Integration Engineering (IIIE. APIs, events, and workflows are modified as opposed to being fixed connectors into decision-making communication channels, where systems exchange intent, not data only. In order to facilitate this, platforms need observable interactions, structured contracts and feedback-sensitive workflows. Integration has ceased to be the issue of delivering information reliably, but rather, the ability to coordinate behavior on the distributed services. Knowledgeable platforms should then have state awareness, semantic communication, and dynamic adaptability in such a way that autonomous components can be safely actively managed within enterprise regulations.

Consequently, enterprise architecture is shifting to collaboration-based design. Goals and policies are defined by humans, and platforms are linked to the coordination of the execution by intelligent agents and interconnected services. The environment that integrates the automation, analytics and decision logic becomes the backbone of integration where the organization can run complex digital ecosystems without commensurate growth in operation effort.

Contract-Driven Design strengthens this by making the interface of an explicit agreement between the service providers and consumers. API specifications define request and response schema, authentication policies, validation policies, error models and versioning policies. These contracts are the authority reference point of development, testing and governance. By implementing the agreed specifications in parallel, teams can develop and prove services at an early stage and eliminate uncertainty and avoid integration setbacks towards the end of the lifecycle.

Subsequently, the enterprise architecture is shifting to collaboration-based design. The objectives and policies set by humans are defined, interaction rules are set by APIs and platforms enable co-ordination using intelligent agents and connected services. The automation, analytics, and decision logic harmonize on the backbone of integration to create the controlled environment. In API-First thinking and discipline based on contracts, enterprises are able to gain scalability, interoperability and architectural stability and make smart, adaptive digital ecosystems accessible.

2.1.1 Benefits of API-First Strategy in Business Environments

The old systems are usually inflexible. Whenever a firm needs to introduce a new facility or collaborate with another platform, it must deal with long integration projects, dependency mapping, and several cycles of cross-environment testing. Any minor updates can involve a coordinated change in databases, services, and user interfaces, making them riskier and slowing their delivery. Any modifications to be made by the teams require them to be informed of the legacy behaviors, a factor that introduces extra time and operational overhead. By developing modular and reusable building blocks that can self-evolve, API-first removes these bottlenecks and can communicate with each other via well-defined interfaces. Organizations display capabilities in structured endpoints rather than changing the entire application even when internal logic is changing. This enables various teams to operate concurrently and be compatible across system.

The benefits are clear:

- **Speed:** The product launching process can be faster, the development process can be shorter, and new services or channels can be experimented with faster. Organizations can make slight changes rather than make big, coordinated releases. This is because parallel development is possible since services interact via explicit contracts as opposed to in-house assumptions.
- **Scalability:** Simple to expand or adjust into different markets, regions, and customer segments with not having to redesign the whole platform. New services may be introduced alongside existing ones, and workloads may be shared across multiple systems without redesigning the core applications.
- **Collaboration:** The fluid integration with partners, vendors, and ecosystems on standard interfaces, where external innovation can be done without internal exposure. External systems communicate through the stable APIs and domestic implementations are not dependent on one another.

This is paradigm-shifting in other industries like banking and finance sectors where a bank can modernize within a very short time without interfering with its stability and going by the legal norms required. The control rules can be put on the interface level such that validation and auditing of the channels would be identical throughout. The old cores are working in the background and the new digital services are being connected with the controlled layers of integration. Companies do not need to re-code their bedrock systems to add mobile platforms, partner ecosystems and new customer experiences. Consequently, the institutions facilitate the growth of digital, ensure the stability of operations, and adapt to evolving market needs without interfering with the services provided.

2.1.2 Operational Framework of the API-First Approach

There are three principles that guide the API-first philosophy:

- **APIs are designed initially:** Teams structure, data models, and functionality of APIs and then create interfaces and logic. The contract is not developed at the end of the process but at the beginning, instead of working on user interfaces or the code behind. This will provide a clear understanding on how systems will interact with each other, what data will be shared and what behavior to expect. Early focus on API specifications helps organizations eliminate ambiguity, align stakeholders and provide a consistent baseline on the parallel development of teams.
- **APIs are products:** They are documented, have version control, and lifecycle management and are consistent over the long run. APIs are also planned, maintained, monitored and enhanced just like any other product. Having them well documented and using versioning techniques to prevent their destabilization by internal and external consumers. Lifecycle management makes sure updates and depreciations and additions are managed in a controlled and predictive fashion. This kind of approach towards products will promote responsibility, utility and environmentally friendly architecture.
- **The entire communication is through APIs:** Internally based tools as well as outside partners will be communicating through the same interfaces with the front-end applications. This kind of standardization removes the dependency behind the scenes and removes the special-case integrations that complicate things. It is through a standardized and controlled interface whether it is a mobile application, analytics engine or third-party vendor consuming a service. This introduces uniformity to the business

and simplifies it to a considerable extent to monitor, apply security, and develop scaling strategies.

The outcome is that the system will allow every level in the business entity to be innovative without interfering with the whole system. The features the teams can make with the already existing services include new features, extensions of the services or introduction of new partners. Systems are constructed and maintained independently and connected with one another through stable contracts. This means that the organization can be more agile, resilient and expand digital activities without compromising the architectural structure.

2.1.3 Classification and Types Of APIS

The API-first approach is broad and recognizes the different kinds of APIs that play specific functions in the ecosystem and serve different integration needs across the enterprise architecture:

1. **Private APIs** - Tie in Systems and enhance productivity. They enable the communication of departments and services in the same organization to use standardized interfaces, rather than accessing databases directly, or using highly integrated attachments. This minimizes dependency conflicts, eases maintenance and allows the teams to upgrade the internal services without impacting other applications. Share capabilities Group capabilities may be accessed securely by internal analytics tools, monitoring platforms, and operational dashboards and controlled boundaries may be maintained.

2. **Partner APIs** - Allows third-party cooperation among organizations. Such interfaces are distributed among the few business partners, vendors or service providers under controlled access policies. Authentication, authorization, and usage agreement is used to make sure that only authorized parties can support certain services. Partner APIs facilitates coordination of the supply chains, payment processing, exchange of data and collaborative provision of services without compromising security and governance concerns. They assist organizations to grow potentials without revealing internal structure.

3. **Public APIs** - Open up the functionality to any 3rd -party developer and create new ecosystems. Applications, extensions or integrations can be developed by external developers based on standard endpoints and documentation. This promotes external innovation within the organization, boosts platform adoption, and value addition via community-based solutions. Public APIs usually consist of rate limits, monitoring, and version management in order to keep the performance and stability at scale.

A smart adapter layer that allows the integration of modern platforms into conventional legacy systems is also an investment by many organizations. This layer has the effect of converting the modern API requests into a form comprehensible by the older infrastructure and translating the legacy responses to the standard outputs. This type of design saves integration work and limits the risk of migration because the old systems can still be active when new services are being deployed. This has meant that old infrastructure does not need to be immediately replaced and on a large scale as it can be integrated with modern innovation.

2.1.4 API-Led Architecture in Enterprise Integration

Enterprise systems usually comprise numerous old-fashioned platforms, third-party services, and external applications that should communicate with one another. These systems often have direct interconnections that form tightly coupled architectures that are hard to maintain and scale. The API-Led Architecture focuses on this problem by grouping APIs into systematic layers that bring about system capabilities in a versatile and reproducible way. Rather than tying applications directly to databases or back services, the communication is provided through more normal APIs that serve as building blocks that can be deployed throughout the enterprise.

The API-Led Architecture is an extension of API-First in that it defines the structure of APIs that should be used within the enterprise ecosystem. Although both API-First and API-Led Architecture tend to design API first and then implement, the latter aims at structuring the API into logical layers to segregate system access, business logic, and user experiences. This multi-layered solution enables organizations to make integration simpler, enhance scalability, and speed up the process of digital innovation.

Three-Layer Model of API-Led Architecture

API-Led Architecture generally follows a three-layer model that separates system connectivity, business logic, and consumer interaction.

1. **System APIs**

   System APIs enable an access control to underlying enterprise systems including databases, ERP systems, legacy applications, and external services. They reveal fundamental information and operations but hide the diversity of the background systems. When there are changes in the underlying technologies of the back-end then, only the System APIs would be required to be changed and other layers will not be impacted.

2. **Process APIs**

   Process APIs are data aggregators and coordinators of information between several System APIs to create business logic and business processes. They constitute the main business skills of an organization. An example is that a Process API can use customer data, payment verification, and inventory information to process the order.

3. **Experience APIs**

   Experience APIs are structured to provide information in a format defined into a particular user interface like mobile apps, web apps, partner applications, or IoT devices. They can customize responses to the requirements of the consuming application as well as without changing the underlying business logic.

Advantages of API-Led Architecture

API-Led Architecture provides several strategic advantages for enterprise integration platforms.

- **Reusability:** APIs developed in one layer can be reused across multiple applications and services.
- **Modularity:** Each layer operates independently, enabling teams to modify systems without affecting other components.

- **Scalability:** New applications or partners can be integrated easily through existing APIs.
- **Governance and Security:** APIs enable centralized policy enforcement, authentication, and monitoring.
- **Faster Innovation:** Organizations can rapidly develop new digital services by assembling capabilities from existing APIs.

It can be used with API-based contract development, in which API specifications are formal contracts among services. Such contracts guarantee that every API layer is predictable and standardized in its communication so that they can be developed and deployed independently in distributed systems.

2.1.5 Key Insights into Contract-Driven Deployment

- Microservices integration can be aided by contract-driven development (or CDD), but it requires a new paradigm of stakeholder participation.
- In contrast to standard procedures, CDD entails creating and archiving API specifications prior to application development, which could take some time to implement.
- In order to improve component testability, CDD builds upon and adds to a robust test pyramid that calls for adjustments to test strategy, composition, and application architecture.
- To demonstrate the benefits of CDD and determine what adjustments to your workflow are required, begin the adoption process with a small number of teams before extending it to others.
- Convince leadership and others to support widespread adoption by providing a seamless onboarding process with contextualized playbooks and CDD tools based on the lessons learned and data from the original proof of concept.

For microservices integration to be successful, contract compatibility between components must now be independently tested early in the SDLC. By using API specifications as executable contracts, contract-driven development offers a convincing solution to this issue. However, selecting

API specifications and/or related tools is only one aspect of contract-driven development. Warming up to the ideas and internalizing the underlying reasoning may take some time.

2.1.6 API Contracts and System Design Principles

API Contracts are agreements between two systems that explain how they will talk to each other using an API. They provide precise definitions for things like the types of data that can be delivered and received, the techniques that can be employed, and the proper way to submit requests. These contracts ensure that everything goes as planned and that both the user and the API provider understand how the API functions.

Let's use a diagram to better understand this:

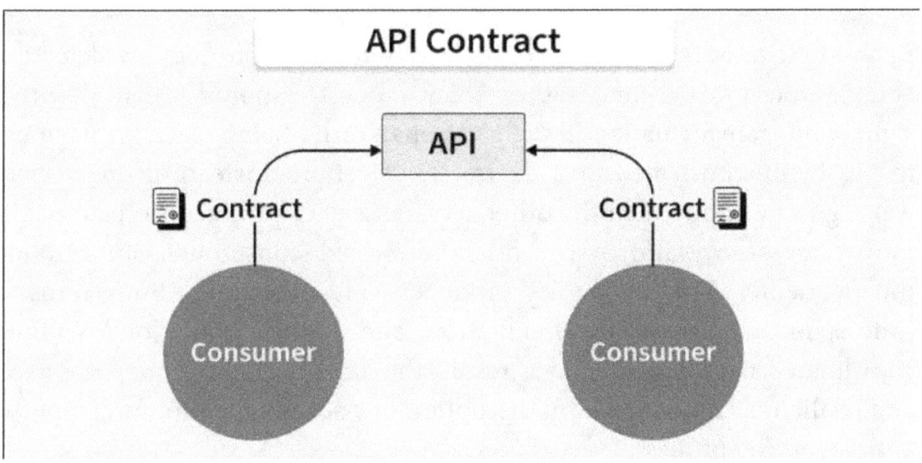

Figure 2.1: API Contract

Source: (GeeksforGeeks, 2025a)

Real-World Examples of API Contracts

- **GitHub API:** This extensive set of endpoints allows users to connect with GitHub's features, including pull requests, problems, and repositories. The methods, parameters, and response formats are all spelt out in detail in the API contract.

- **Stripe API:** Comprehensive documentation on endpoints for managing payments, clients, subscriptions, and more is included in Stripe's payment processing API. Response formats, error handling, and necessary and optional arguments are all outlined in the contract. Stripe's API documentation is renowned for being thorough and easy to understand.
- **Twitter API:** This tool enables developers to use Twitter's functions, including searching, following, and tweeting. The endpoints, methods, parameters, and response formats are described in the API contract.

2.2 EVENT-DRIVEN ARCHITECTURES AND MESSAGING PLATFORMS

EDA employs systems that are organized in terms of production, detection and response to events, rather than request-response calls. Event A significant transformation in the form of an order being placed, a payment that is being confirmed or a device status report. Instead of one service waiting in harmony with the other service, service producers create events into a message platform to which interested consumers can respond independently. This decouples producers and consumers both across a time span and across implementation, and systems can evolve without coordinated deployments. As a result, the apps become more responsive and resilient as the short-term disruption of a service will not interrupt the entire working process.

Messaging platforms are the foundation on which this model of communication can be attained. They are used to perform the role of routing, buffering and dependable delivery of events in distributed environments. The messages are either sent through one or more queues to be processed on a point-to-point fashion or sent through topics and streams to be consumed by a number of services. These systems have features of persistence, retries, ordering, and delivery acknowledgements to make sure that key business happenings are not lost when failures occur. Messaging infrastructure can achieve scaling of a service, spike tolerance, and asynchronous workload processing across other systems, thus removing communication from computation and preventing the collapse of reliant systems.

Systems are responsive to business operations as they happen and not based on periodic synchronization or batch execution. This aids in upholding protracted workflows, reactive automation and ongoing data propagation across analysis and operational frameworks. Event streams can be a good source of truth to distributed operations when they are used with adequate schema governance and monitoring. The architecture then evolves more towards the loosely coordinated collaboration instead of the tightly coordinated control flows to better the scalability, fault tolerance and adaptability to the dynamically operating environments.

2.2.1 OPERATIONAL MECHANICS OF EVENT-DRIVEN ARCHITECTURE

A software design pattern called "event-driven architecture" (EDA) makes it possible to build loosely linked, scalable systems. The flow is driven by events that indicate occurrences or changes in the system. Asynchronously, interested components consume them after they are created by several sources and published to an event bus or message broker. This strategy encourages adaptability, scalability, and durability.

By utilizing strategies like event sourcing and CQRS (Command and Query Responsibility Segregation: a pattern that isolates read and update activities for a data store, for increased performance, scalability, and security), event-driven systems take advantage of eventual consistency. By capturing all system state changes as a series of events, event sourcing makes it possible to recreate the system at any time. By separating read and write processes, CQRS allows for consistent and effective querying.

Scalability, flexible coupling, and autonomous system component development and deployment are some advantages of EDA. It manages real-time event processing, event-driven integrations, and intricate workflows.

Systems become scalable by adopting event-driven design, which enables them to respond to events independently and asynchronously. Additionally, the design uses strategies like event versioning, idempotency, and compensating actions to address issues with data consistency.

All things considered, event-driven architecture offers durability, scalability, and flexibility, which makes it appropriate for contemporary applications including intricate workflows, real-time event processing, and event-driven connections.

2.2.2 Real-World Implementations of Event-Driven Architecture

Nearly actual examples of EDA contain:

1. **E-commerce Order Processing:** n event is started to start inventory control, payment processing, and delivery coordination when a customer puts an order.
2. **Internet of Things (IoT) Data Collection:** When sensor data reaches a predetermined threshold, IoT devices trigger events, allowing for real-time monitoring and analysis for a range of applications.
3. **User Registration & Authentication:** Events are started when a user registers or logs in in order to update user profiles, validate credentials, and provide access to various system resources.
4. **Notification System:** Events update pertinent users via email, SMS, or push notifications when certain circumstances are met, such as when new messages are received or tasks are issued.
5. **Stock Market Trading:** When market conditions change, events are generated to trigger automated trading strategies, enabling real-time execution of buy/sell orders.
6. **Real-Time Analytics:** When data streams are received, events are set off, enabling ongoing analysis and the creation of insights, such as tracking website traffic or identifying fraudulent activity.
7. **Workflow Management:** Events are set off to advance the workflow when a task is finished or a milestone is reached, guaranteeing smooth cooperation and process automation.
8. **Sensor Integration in Smart Homes:** When sensors pick up motion, temperature changes, or door openings, they create events that cause things like lights to switch on or thermostat settings to alter.

9. **Event-Driven Microservices:** Systems that are loosely linked and scalable are made possible by the usage of events to facilitate communication between many microservices.
10. **Online Gaming:** Players can engage in real time and synchronize their games by doing activities like moving characters or finishing missions, which trigger events.

2.2.3 Advantages of Event-Driven Architecture

The primary benefits of event-driven architecture include enhanced scalability and agility, as well as real-time insights, connectivity, and responses. Scaling, meeting contemporary business requirements, and guaranteeing real-time connection across vital applications and systems are all practically unachievable without EDA.

The following are the main benefits of event-driven architecture:

- **Loose Coupling and Scalability**

  By using events to decouple components, EDA encourages loose connectivity between them. Asynchronous event messages allow components in EDA to communicate with one another, allowing for autonomous development, deployment, and scaling. The system can be more modular, flexible, and agile because to this loose connection. Scalability and adaptability to shifting business needs are made possible by the capacity to add or change new components without affecting the ones that already exist.

- **Real-time Processing and Responsiveness**

  EDA responds to events as they happen, allowing for real-time processing and responsiveness. Events are recorded and processed almost instantly, including user interactions, system alerts, and outside triggers. This guarantees the system's ability to react swiftly to modifications, facilitating prompt response, real-time analytics, and quicker decision-making. EDA is especially well-suited for use cases like financial systems, Internet of Things applications, or real-time monitoring where responsiveness and real-time data processing are essential.

- **Reliability and Fault Tolerance**

  EDA uses event-driven communication to improve fault tolerance and system reliability. An audit trail of previous events can be created by logging events and keeping them in a durable event storage. This guarantees fault tolerance and system resilience by enabling error management, recovery, and event replay. A dependable and consistent system can be achieved by replaying the events to return components to a consistent state in the event of a breakdown.

- **Seamless Integration with Disparate Systems**

  EDA makes it easier to integrate many technologies and systems. Components can exchange information and initiate actions across many systems since they communicate through events. Because different systems can consume and output events regardless of their underlying technologies or programming languages, this facilitates effective data sharing and interoperability. EDA facilitates the development of event-driven architectures that include cloud services, legacy systems, third-party apps, and microservices.

  All things considered, event-driven architecture offers technological benefits that enable businesses to create adaptable, scalable, responsive, and dependable systems. EDA makes it possible to create reliable and flexible systems that can satisfy the requirements of contemporary applications by adopting loose coupling, real-time processing, fault tolerance, and seamless integration.

2.2.4 Limitations and Challenges of Event-Driven Architecture

EDA has certain drawbacks despite its many advantages. Let's investigate them:

1. **Complexity:** In contrast to conventional monolithic systems, EDA adds more complexity. The complexity of the system as a whole may rise due to the need for event producers, event consumers, event brokers, and other elements.

2. **Event Ordering**: In an event-driven system, maintaining the proper sequence of occurrences can be difficult. Certain use cases, such financial transactions or data consistency, may need maintaining precise event ordering, which calls for careful planning and execution.

3. **Eventual Consistency:** It might be challenging to achieve event consistency across several services or components in distributed systems. It might be difficult to maintain data integrity and make sure that all pertinent systems are appropriately updated in reaction to events. The same issues affect EDA-based architectures.

4. **Debugging and Troubleshooting:** Compared to conventional request-response systems, event-driven systems can be more difficult to diagnose and identify problems with. It can be difficult to follow the chain of events and pinpoint the underlying source of issues because they can set off a sequence of reactions across multiple components.

2.2.5 Selection of Optimal Messaging Platforms

The requirements of your company will determine which messaging platform is best. Here are five important factors to think about.

1. **The breadth of channels—and the breadth of features available on those channels**

   Customers have long desired a variety of channels, according to consumer feedback, but there is no one-size-fits-all solution for the ideal balance of communications channels. The needs of the company and your clients will determine this.

   Industry-specific messaging preferences may differ. Customers are increasingly adopting social media to communicate with grocery stores, while text messaging is the preferred method for remote work and learning platforms. Additionally, chatbots are being used by almost half of the insurance and banking companies to enable large-scale client self-service.

The channels that your clients spend the most time on must also be taken into account. It makes sense to provide live chat or in-app messaging if you have a mobile app so users can receive assistance without leaving the app.

Finding a messaging platform that enables you to reach your clients wherever they are and effortlessly add or remove channels as their needs evolve is crucial. Businesses with a keen understanding of messaging take into account both current and future mediums. Additionally, without the appropriate messaging provider, adding new channels can be challenging.

The range of rich, natively supported functionalities that are accessible on a messaging platform's channels is equally as significant as the number of channels it offers: Rich channel features and a broad selection of channel access are not provided by all providers.

Rich features boost conversions and consumer engagement. Rich message kinds, such as carousels, forms, and picklists, allow businesses to stand out from the competition by enabling customers to act within the messenger, such as scheduling appointments, making reservations, or completing payments.

2. **How much context your business will have at its fingertips**

   Being present wherever your customers are is only one aspect of omnichannel marketing. A company must locate a messaging platform that allows it to go one step further and construct a single, cohesive profile of its client, complete with context and conversation history that transfers across channels. Customers can now easily navigate between channels without having to repeatedly enter their ticket number or mailing address while waiting on hold or bouncing between departments.

3. **The agent's experience, including the tools your support team will have to manage conversations**

   Yes, support staff require an omnichannel user interface to respond to discussions at the front end, but having the tools to manage those conversations at scale on the back end is just as crucial. The challenge is that not many messaging services deliver both a fantastic agent experience and an easy developer experience.

Businesses need a method to centrally define rules of engagement and streamline handoffs between people, automation, and AI throughout the organization as they implement chatbots, automation, and multi-departmental messaging infrastructure. Agents may reduce time-to-resolution, save support resources, and streamline customer-facing interactions with the use of triggers, automations, and processes that extend beyond ticket-based routing.

4. **Your use case**

The ideal messaging platform is one that can be programmed and customised to meet the demands of your company. Here are some instances and topics to think about:

How many participants will you need in a single conversation?

Several people from both inside and outside the company are frequently involved in modern customer connections. Companies that run marketplaces will probably have to link riders and drivers as well as buyers and dealers. Finding a messaging service that is also effective at one-to-many communication is crucial, as the majority only offer one-to-one communication.

Do you plan to offer self-service?

Customers may find answers on their own, in context, and at any time of day thanks to businesses' large-scale integration of chatbots for self-service. To prevent customers from leaving their carts because they have unanswered enquiries, an online retailer can include a chatbot on their checkout page. Instead of being restricted to a particular set of integrations or capabilities, businesses should seek out a messaging provider that allows them to launch a bot across multiple channels and is bot and AI agnostic, meaning that it gives them the freedom to do whatever they want in the conversation, on their terms.

How can you brand the messaging experience?

Using rich content types like GIFs and location sharing, you can create in-app messaging on any platform, including web, Android, and iOS, to increase user engagement with the products and services your consumers use on a daily basis.

5. **How the solution fits with your current infrastructure—and will allow you to scale in the future**

   Selecting an open platform that enables your company to adapt swiftly and follow your clients wherever they go next is crucial. A smooth client experience depends on both initial and ongoing time-to-value. The perfect messaging platform can be set up to accommodate any workflow, is strong enough to manage the most complicated operations, and is adaptable enough to grow at any rate.

   Whether it's bots, natural language processing, automation, reporting, or analytics, an open and adaptable solution also makes it simple to integrate with new technologies, channels, and third parties your company adds in the future. As your company grows, this guarantees that the marketing, sales, and support departments stay in sync rather than operating independently, freeing up their time to assist clients instead of managing a system.

2.3 REST, GRAPHQL, GRPC, AND ASYNC APIS

Representational State Transfer API is referred to as REST API. This kind of API (Application Programming Interface) enables online connection across many platforms. REST APIs function by having the client and server exchange requests and responses, usually in JSON format.

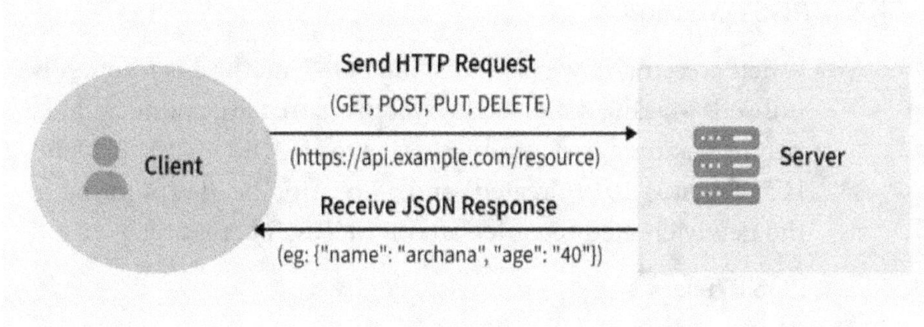

Figure 2.2: Rest API

Source: (GeeksforGeeks, 2025b)

- One of the HTTP methods is used to send a request from the client to the server via a web URL.
- The requested resource, which may be HTML, XML, an image, or JSON—JSON being the most widely used format for contemporary web services—is then returned by the server.
- These methods map to CRUD operations (Create, Read, Update, Delete) for managing resources on the web.

2.3.1 Common HTTP Methods in Restful APIs

POST, GET, PUT, PATCH, and DELETE are the five HTTP methods that are frequently utilized in a REST-based architecture. CRUD (create, read, update, and delete) actions are represented by these, respectively. Other techniques, such as OPTIONS and HEAD, are less commonly employed.

1. **GET Method**

   To read (or retrieve) a representation of a resource, use the HTTP GET technique. When using the safe path, GET delivers an HTTP response code of 200 (OK) along with a representation in either XML or JSON. It typically returns a 404 (NOT FOUND) or 400 (BAD REQUEST) in an error scenario.

   GET /users/123

   This request retrieves information for user ID 123.

2. **POST Method**

When creating new resources, the POST method is frequently utilised. Making subordinate resources that are connected to a parent resource is a common usage for it. The server delivers HTTP status 201 (Created) and a Location header pointing to the newly created resource after a successful creation.

```
POST /users
{
 "name": "Anjali",
 "email": "gfg@example.com"
}
```

With the information provided, a new user is created by this request.

3. **PUT Method**

A resource on the server can be created or updated using the PUT HTTP method. PUT replaces the existing resource at the given URL by sending the complete resource in the request body. It can generate a new resource if the existing one isn't available.

```
PUT /users/123
{
 "name": "Anjali",
 "email": "gfg@example.com"
}
```

This request either creates a new user if none already exists or updates the user with ID 123.

4. **PATCH Method**

A resource on the server can be partially updated using the PATCH HTTP technique. In contrast to PUT, PATCH just requires the request body to contain the fields that need to be modified. Instead of replacing the full resource, it alters some portions of it.

```
PATCH /users/123
{
    "email": "new.email@example.com"
}
```

Only the email address of the user with ID 123 is updated by this request; all other user information remains unaltered.

5. **DELETE Method**

   It is used to delete a resource identified by a URI. Provide a response content and HTTP status 200 (OK) upon successful deletion.

   DELETE /users/123

   This request deletes the user with ID 123.

2.3.2 Architectural Overview of GRAPHQL APIs

Clients can communicate with a single endpoint using the GraphQL query language for APIs to obtain the precise data they require without chaining queries together. By lowering the frequency of round trips between the client and the server, this method can enhance performance.

Compared to REST and SOAP, scheme access with access to a wide range of schema objects and properties makes digital resources available by use of web APIs more flexible and powerful with GraphQL. Moreover, GraphQL does not send data to the client which was not demanded, making it more efficient with a less amount of transferred data. These advantages have resulted in GraphQL gaining a huge popularity growth in recent years.

The use of modern applications such as AI systems depends on discoverable, consistent and structured APIs. REST contributed to the standardization of our API construction, but as the data flows get more complicated, teams need a model that can evolve fast.

GraphQL provides such flexibility. It specifies a common scheme between the clients and servers, enabling exact queries, foreseeable response, and more effective data transfer. For organizations scaling their API ecosystems or preparing APIs for agent-driven workloads, GraphQL represents a natural next step.

2.3.3 Understanding the Tradeoff Analysis Between GRAPHQL and Rest

An "architectural concept" for network-based applications is a REST API. In contrast, GraphQL is a collection of tools and a query language that uses a single endpoint. In recent years, GraphQL has primarily been used to maximize flexibility and performance, whereas REST has been used to develop new APIs.

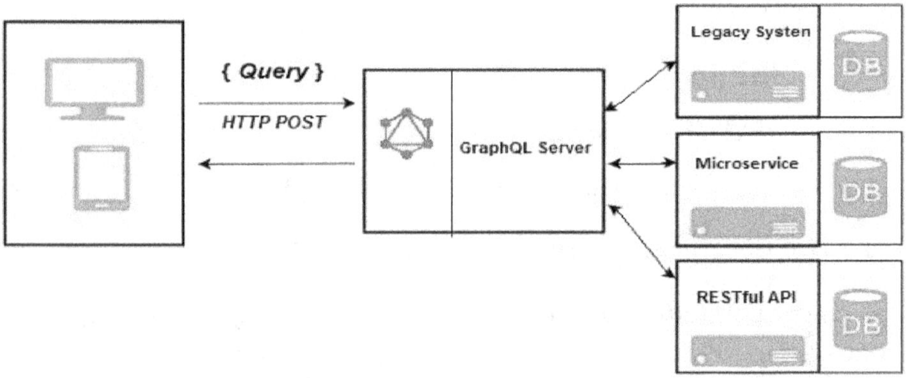

Figure 2.3: GraphQL Architecture

Source: (Batra, 2025)

You will always receive complete "datasets" while using REST. You would need to make x REST API requests in order to obtain information from x objects. Your requests may look like this if you're asking for product details for an eCommerce website:

Make a single request for product information, including names, descriptions, etc.

In a separate request, ask for the prices associated with that product.

Request pictures from a different dataset for product photos.

Everything you requested will still be provided, but it will take multiple requests, and depending on how the content/data was organized at each endpoint, each dataset may bring you a tonne of extra information you didn't need or want, like reviews, variations, discounts, etc. On the one hand, this is quite straightforward—you have a single endpoint that performs a single function, making it simple to comprehend and control. To put it another way, X data is provided by X endpoints.

On the other hand, you cannot restrict the fields that the REST API delivers if you wish to collect data from a certain endpoint; you will always receive the entire data set, or over fetching.

From many objects to particular fields within each entity, GraphQL's query language allows you to customize the request to your exact specifications. GraphQL can accomplish a lot with the information it receives from the X endpoint, but you must first specify your needs.

Using the same example, the request would only need to retrieve Product Name, product Description, product Image, and product Price from the same endpoint in a single request. Over-fetching would not be a problem because all other database content would not be returned.

Aspect	REST	GraphQL
Endpoints	Multiple resource endpoints	Single /graphql endpoint
Data fetching	Server defines response shape	Client defines response shape
Over-fetching	Common	None; client requests only needed fields
Versioning	Managed via URL (/v1, /v2)	Evolved via schema; no breaking changes
Caching	Built into HTTP	Custom or layer-specific caching
Real-time data	Requires separate setup	Built-in with subscriptions

GraphQL provides flexibility and efficiency, whereas REST offers simplicity and predictable caching. Many organizations use both REST and GraphQL to provide stable, reusable APIs and dynamic, user-facing experiences.

2.3.4 Conceptual Foundations of gRPC

Let's first explain RPC in order to comprehend gRPC. Software programs employ RPC, an inter-process communication technique, to interact over a network. gRPC is based on RPC and communicates via HTTP/2, a transport layer protocol. Because gRPC is RPC-based, clients can call any of its service methods, regardless of whether they are operating on a local computer or a distant server. Because of this, it is a flexible tool that can be used for more than just GET and PUT queries.

Protocol Buffers (protobuf) are used by gRPC as the interface defining language for the API interface rather than JSON or XML. The protobuf compiler transforms the data structures that developers construct to specify the message format between the client and the server into a binary format called protobuf.

Key Components of gRPC

- Protocol buffers are a method for serialising structured data that is independent of language.
- HTTP/2: The foundational transport protocol that offers functions like header compression and multiplexing.
- Channel: An address and port connection to a gRPC server.
- Stub: An object on the client side that uses the same methods as the gRPC server.

Today, the majority of APIs are accessed via the widely used HTTP protocol, and Representational State Transfer (REST) is the framework used to develop these APIs. We refer to these APIs as RESTful APIs.

However, you have probably heard about gRPC if you have spent the last few years working in API development. A strong, more recent framework for creating APIs and putting their communication into practice is called gRPC. The goal of this CNCF incubation project is to offer a cutting-edge, open-source framework that can be used anywhere and is based on Remote Procedure Calls (RPC).

gRPC, which was created by Google and made available as an open-source project in 2015, is becoming more and more well-liked in the microservices community since it provides a more straightforward and effective substitute for REST. The work done on Stubby, Google's internal RPC framework, served as its foundation. gRPC is used in the systems of many of the biggest corporations in the world, such as Netflix, Cisco, Twitter, and Uber.

What makes up gRPC?

Let's first explain RPC in order to comprehend gRPC. Software programs employ RPC, an inter-process communication technique, to interact over a network. gRPC is based on RPC and communicates via HTTP/2, a transport layer protocol. Because gRPC is RPC-based, clients can call any of its service methods, regardless of whether they are operating on a local computer or a distant server. Because of this, it is a flexible tool that can be used for more than just GET and PUT queries.

Protocol Buffers (protobuf) are used by gRPC as the interface defining language for the API interface rather than JSON or XML. The protobuf compiler transforms the data structures that developers construct to specify the message format between the client and the server into a binary format called protobuf.

Key Components of gRPC

- **Protocol buffers:** Protocol buffers are a method for serialising structured data that is independent of language.
- **HTTP/2:** The foundational transport protocol that offers functions like header compression and multiplexing.
- **Channel:** An address and port connection to a gRPC server.
- **Stub:** An object on the client side that uses the same methods as the gRPC server.

2.3.5 Operational Workflow of gRPC

Creating gRPC services with methods that clients can call is how gRPC APIs are implemented. A contract between a client and a server is then defined. The procedures that customers can invoke from the service, the parameters that can be supplied to those processes, and the kinds of data that will be returned are all outlined in this contract. In order to call the processes and exchange data, the client and server utilise this contract to produce code in their respective languages. All communication-related features, including error handling, network calls, and message serialization, are covered by this created code.

As previously stated, gRPC serializes messages using Protocol Buffers and transports via HTTP/2. The client invokes the API methods locally after creating local objects or stubs for them. Client requests are sent to the remote server by the gRPC runtime, which also gets the answers.

gRPC API Service Methods

Four different kinds of service methods are supported by gRPC:

1. **Unary RPC:** One input and one output are returned by a unary service method.

2. **Server Streaming RPC:** A server streaming service method sends a stream of outputs after receiving one input from the client. Additionally, it can return several outputs as new data becomes available.

3. **Client Streaming RPC:** Client streaming services establish a connection with a server, after which the client side can start delivering data until the server approves the start of the stream.

4. **Bidirectional Streaming RPC:** Bidirectional streaming services send and receive data streams in both directions at the same time

Every kind of approach has special advantages and applications. For instance, simple RPCs are best served by unary techniques, whereas tasks needing a lot of data processing are best served by server streaming methods. Bidirectional streaming techniques are ideal for real-time communication, while client streaming techniques can be employed when latency is an issue.

2.3.6 Practical use Cases for gRPC

You might choose to design your APIs using the gRPC framework for a number of reasons.

1. **Broad language support**

   gRPC supports a wide range of languages. The majority of contemporary languages and frameworks, such as Java, Ruby, Go, Node.js, Python, C#, and PHP, support it extensively. As previously stated, gRPC clients are more flexible than typical APIs because they can call any function—just GET.

2. **Smaller message size**

   Because binary message formats, or Protocol Buffers, are smaller and easier to interpret than text-based formats like JSON, gRPC messages are smaller than those of typical RESTful APIs. Faster transmission between the client and the server is the outcome of this.

3. **Faster communication**

   Because HTTP/2 is more efficient than older protocols like HTTP/1.1, gRPC can lower latency and use less network traffic. Additionally, the communications can go between servers and clients faster because they are smaller. Additionally, it makes the user experience more seamless and less taxing on the network.

4. **Streaming Connection**

   Support for streaming connection mode is another benefit of gRPC. When data is too big to send or receive all at once, performance can be enhanced by using streaming mode, which sends or receives data in chunks. This eliminates the need for clients to wait for the full response to come and enables them to receive data from the server continually. Users are therefore spared from having to wait for the entire data transfer to be finished.

   No data is lost or corrupted during transmission because the client-server connection is maintained throughout streaming. For real-time applications like gaming or chat, gRPC streaming is perfect.

5. **Pluggable Support**

   Plugging in load balancing, tracing, health checks, and authentication are all supported by gRPC. This facilitates the setup and administration of high-performance systems. Because gRPC is modular, configuring its various feature sets is easy.

6. **Strong Typing**

   Protocol buffers, which offer robust message typing, are used by gRPC. This can result in more resilient and dependable systems by identifying faults at compile time instead of runtime.

7. **Code Generation**

   Using your service definitions, gRPC automatically creates client and server code. The amount of boilerplate code you have to develop and maintain might be greatly decreased as a result.

2.3.7 Core Components of ASYNC APIs

There are two essential components: communication protocols and mechanisms.

1. **Communication protocols**

   These non-blocking APIs use various protocols for communication, such as:

   - **Advanced Message Queuing Protocol (AMQP)** — AMPQ enables asynchronous communication between producers and consumers.
   - **Message Queuing Telemetry Transport (MQTT)** — MQTT is a protocol for sending data to and from devices and networks with limited bandwidth. It uses the pub/sub messaging model and is ideal for small sensors and mobile devices.
   - **WebSockets** — A WebSocket is a bidirectional communication protocol that sends and receives data in real time between the client and the server. It sends

information using a single Transmission Control Protocol (TCP) connection.

- **Server-Sent Events (SSE)** — With SSE, the server sends or pushes automatic updates to the client in real time via an HTTP connection.

2. **Mechanisms**

Async APIs use mechanisms to specify what should happen once asynchronous operations have been completed:

- **Callbacks** — Callbacks are functions passed to other functions as arguments when an asynchronous operation is done. Developers often avoid using many callbacks when implementing async APIs to prevent "callback hell" or the "pyramid of doom." Instead, they rely on promises to handle callbacks.
- **Promises** — An object that symbolizes the three states of an operation—pending, fulfilled, and rejected—is called a promise. It is given back when an asynchronous operation is successful or unsuccessful. With a promise, you attach callbacks instead of passing them into a function.
- **Futures** — Futures are read-only objects representing potential future values resulting from asynchronous operations or computations. Most languages support callbacks and promises, but only some support futures, such as Python, Scala, Rust, and Dart.

These components are core to how async APIs work. You need to combine them carefully to ensure that your application performs well.

2.3.8 Comparative Analysis: Synchronous Vs. Asynchronous APIs

You can use both synchronous and asynchronous APIs to build applications that perform tasks in real time. The trick is knowing when to use asynchronous APIs, synchronous APIs, or a combination. Here's a quick compare-and-contrast exercise:

	Synchronous APIs	**Asynchronous APIs**
Blocking	The client must wait for the API to respond before executing other tasks (blocking).	The client can perform other tasks while waiting for the API to respond (non-blocking).
Execution	Requests are handled one at a time in order (sequential).	Multiple requests are handled simultaneously (concurrent).
Implementation	Linear, predictable execution. Generally simpler to implement and manage than async APIs.	Typically involve event loops and callbacks or promises. More complex to implement and maintain than synchronous APIs.
Performance	Tend to run slower when handling long-running tasks, compared to async APIs.	Usually perform better than synchronous APIs, especially when performing multiple asynchronous requests.
Scalability	Each request is handled separately instead of concurrently, limiting scalability.	Can process multiple requests concurrently, facilitating scalability.
Use cases	Ideal for quick and simple tasks. Great for tasks that require immediate feedback and low latency.	Ideal for long-running tasks and high-traffic scenarios. Great for applications that require real-time updates and can tolerate high latency.

2.4 VERSIONING, GOVERNANCE, AND LIFECYCLE MANAGEMENT

Versioning is the process of creating and overseeing several product releases that are enhanced, upgraded, or customized while maintaining the same overall purpose. Versioning is most commonly used in relation to operating systems, software artefacts, and online services, however many developers and suppliers use the term in diverse contexts.

For instance, a continuous series of product versions, like Windows 10 and Windows 11, can be given distinct names or particular numerical identities by suppliers. Various iterations of the same software or application are represented by the numbers, which rise to reflect the most recent advancements and releases (Myerson, 2001).

Versioning enables software development teams to monitor modifications they make to the project code. New features, functionality, or bug fixes can be among the modifications. In a similar way, small changes can also be monitored. On the basis of advancements over several versions, completely new features and functionalities are occasionally offered.

Versioning, also known as software versioning workflow, is an internal activity that helps engineers monitor the growth of their code. Teams working on the project may use internal versioning numbers during development, which might be increased multiple times in a single day. On the other hand, the version that is made public typically doesn't change very often. For example, the development teams use 1.5.0 as the internal version number for Java SE 5.0.

2.4.1 Principles of API Versioning

Documentation versioning is a critical practice that ensures documentation remains synchronized with product development cycles and user needs. As software products evolve through multiple releases, each version may introduce new features, modify existing functionality, or deprecate certain elements, making version-specific documentation essential for user success.

Key Features

- Parallel maintenance of multiple documentation versions corresponding to product releases
- Version-specific content that reflects feature availability and functionality
- Clear version labeling and navigation systems for users

- Automated or streamlined processes for creating new documentation versions
- Archive management for legacy versions with defined retention policies

Benefits for Documentation Teams

- Improved user experience through accurate, version-relevant information
- Reduced support tickets by providing precise documentation for each product version
- Enhanced team efficiency through structured content management workflows
- Better collaboration between documentation and development teams
- Simplified maintenance of legacy product support

Common Misconceptions

- Versioning requires duplicating entire documentation sets for minor changes
- Only major releases need separate documentation versions
- Version management is too complex for small documentation teams
- All content must be versioned equally, regardless of relevance to product changes

2.4.2 Lifecycle Management Framework

The strategic actions taken to effectively advance a product through its entire lifecycle are referred to as lifecycle management. (For this reason, it is also frequently called "product lifecycle management.") Sales, marketing, and product management are just a few of the teams and verticals inside a firm that must contribute to effective lifecycle management.

How experts in these departments perform their duties can be significantly impacted by the stage of a product's lifecycle to which it belongs. For instance, the marketing team must design an advertising campaign that conveys a significant amount of information to the general public and target consumers, such as the functions, advantages, and advantages of a product that has recently been introduced to the market. Conversely, more developed products with a longer and more established track record in the market don't need to be reintroduced to the public; instead, their marketing campaigns should concentrate more on setting them apart from rivals or improving their reputation in a positive way.

Generally speaking, lifecycle management comprises not only determining the stage at which a product is in its lifespan but also acting upon that evaluation and letting it guide the development and advancement of a business's positioning, marketing, and sales activities.

2.4.3 Stages of Product Lifecycle

Since the mid-1900s, people have been analyzing commercial products in terms of their distinct "life stages." Introduction, growth, maturity, saturation, and decline are the five stages of a product's lifecycle, according to a 1957 thesis first put forth by renowned advertising firm Booz Allen Hamilton.

- **Introduction:** A commodity is released into the market after completing the primary phases of product development, which include conception, prototyping, testing, and commercialization.
- **Growth:** The product starts making sales, building a clientele, and bringing in money for the business. As marketing and word-of-mouth acquire traction and the product establishes a reputation within its target market, demand for the product may rise steadily or even quickly during this phase.
- **Maturity:** One could consider this phase to be the "prime" of the product's life. When a commodity reaches the maturity phase, it has a stable client base, consistently makes money for its maker and distributors who sell directly to consumers, and is well-established in its particular market, possibly even gaining a sizable market share. In general, the maturity period of a product is when the maximum sales volumes occur.

- **Saturation:** The saturation stage, as the name suggests, is the phase of a product's lifespan when it has achieved its maximum sales and client capacity. Plateauing sales volumes are one of the most telling indicators that a commodity has reached the saturation stage. This indicates that the product is not growing its clientele. The establishment and entrenchment of competitors who have introduced comparable items is another important external element in the saturation stage. These competitors have penetrated a limited market and made it very difficult for fresh growth to occur.
- **Decline:** When sales of a product start to diminish in a significant and mostly permanent manner, it is inevitable that its standing as an important, high-grossing commodity will decline. The emergence of newer, more sophisticated technology is one of several events and trends that might cause a product to decline. This situation is particularly concerning in the field of electronic components, where new technologies are constantly being developed and causing older goods to become less useful, which leads to discontinuance and obsolescence.

2.4.4 Foundations of Governance in Enterprise Organizations

Enterprise governance can be defined as the mechanism of structures, policies, processes, and controls that can be used to give direction to an organization and its management. It determines the authority to make decisions, evaluation of the decision made and accountability. Fundamentally, governance provides balance between strategic goals, operational performance, risk management, and firm expectations. Governance brings the discipline required to keep large enterprises out of fragmentation, efforts duplication and risk exposure uncontrolled. In its absence, even technically powerful organizations may be affected by erratic priorities, lack of clarity of responsibilities, and ineffective supervision.

One of the aspects of enterprise governance is the clarity of decision-rights. This involves the role definition between boards, executive management, functional heads, and function teams. There are well-defined governance structures that set up the escalations, levels of approval and performance accountability. As an example, the financial governance defines processes of budgeting authority and capital allocation whereas IT governance defines technology investment priorities, architecture standards, and data protection requirements. Ambiguity of decision rights usually leads to delays and conflict in enterprises and wastage of resources. Effective governance will minimize such inefficiencies through formalization of responsibility without needless decelerating innovation.

The other basic dimension is risk overseeing. Businesses exist in an uncertain environment that has regulatory compliance, market uncertainties, cybercrime, and reputation risks. Governance structures incorporate the identification, assessment, and mitigation of risks and reporting of the same in the executive decision making. This encompasses the compliance programs, internal audit system, policy enforcement mechanism, and performance monitoring system. Governance does not eradicate risk, but quantifies risk-taking so that it is a measured and informed process in line with the organizational strategy. In established businesses, risk governance is integrated into planning processes, and it is not an exception

Lastly, enterprise governance facilitates sustainability and ethical behaviour. It sets standards of transparency, reporting, and codes of conduct, which determine the organizational culture. Governance models tend to embrace environmental, social and governance (ESG) factors, stakeholder participation practices as well as nonfinancial performance indicators. In complex organizations, governance brings sanity through the institutionalization of accountability and oversight, but it also provides flexibility within a set of predetermined limits. Enterprise governance offers a disciplined and responsive method of growth enabling organizations to respond responsively in regard to integrity and resiliency in case of high practice.

2.4.5 The Importance of Governance in The Modern Business Environment

Corporate governance is more than just a legal requirement in today's cutthroat and dynamic economic environment; it is a crucial framework for boosting market confidence, encouraging competition, and promoting sustainable growth. An organization can generate long-term value for its stakeholders and shareholders by being accountable, transparent, and responsible, which is ensured by good governance.

An organization may suffer serious repercussions from poor governance. These consist of:

- **Financial loss:** Fraud, resource misallocation, and operational inefficiencies can arise from poor supervision and decision-making.
- **Reputational harm**: A lack of openness or moral behaviour can erode confidence, which can result in a decline in investor and customer support.
- **Regulatory penalties**: Failure to comply with legal and regulatory obligations may result in hefty fines and penalties that harm the company's reputation and financial viability.

2.5 SERVICE MESH AND INTEGRATION GATEWAYS

A software application's service mesh is a specialized infrastructure layer that manages inter-service communication. By abstracting these complexities from individual services, a service mesh can manage traffic routing, security, observability, and resilience tasks.

Modern applications rely on services that communicate with each other. Recall your most recent internet shopping experience. You may have browsed products using the site's search bar. A service is represented by that search. It's possible that you added an item to your online shopping cart or saw suggestions for related products. Additionally, those are also services. The product webpage, which in turn needs to communicate with the user's online shopping cart, must communicate with the inventory database. Additionally, the merchant may offer an in-app product recommendation service. In addition to communicating with the same inventory database that the product page required, this service will interact with a database of product tags in order to provide recommendations.

This is how modern programs are frequently deconstructed: as a network of services, each of which carries out a particular task. One service may need to request data from multiple other services in order to perform its role. However, what happens if certain services—like the retailer's inventory database—are inundated with requests? A service mesh is useful in this situation because it controls communication between services and maximizes the efficiency of all the moving components.

2.5.1 How Service Mesh Works

A data plane and a control plane are used by a service mesh to regulate communication between services. Applications in whatever architecture have always required rules to explain how requests flow from point A to point B; service mesh does not add new capability to an application's runtime environment. A service mesh differs in that it abstracts the logic controlling service-to-service communication from individual services to a layer of infrastructure.

An application incorporates a service mesh as a collection of network proxies to accomplish this. It's likely that you have already used a proxy if you are viewing this page from a work computer. This is how it operates:

- Your company's web proxy received your request for this page as it was sent out.
- It was routed to the server hosting this page after overcoming the security precaution of the proxy.
- This page was then sent back to the proxy, where it was once more examined in relation to its security protocols.
- After that, you received it from the proxy.

Every service instance in a service mesh is matched with a "sidecar" proxy, which operates concurrently with each service and intercepts all network traffic, including inbound and outbound. Every sidecar proxy routes requests to and from other proxies while residing next to a microservice. The proxy handles tasks like traffic routing, load balancing, enforcing security policies, and collecting telemetry data. Instead of communicating directly with one another, services send requests through their sidecar. The sidecars handle inter-service communication. All of this comprises the data plane.

The data plane's configuration and policy distribution are overseen by the control plane. In addition, the control plane gathers telemetry, configures components to enforce policies, distributes traffic routing rules, and maintains security certificates among services.

2.5.2 Benefits of Service Mesh Architecture

Every new instance of an existing service operating in a container or service introduced to an application creates more points of failure and complicates the communication environment. Without a service mesh, it can be very difficult to identify issues in a complicated microservices architecture.

There are several advantages to using a service mesh, including:

- **Improved security.** A service mesh uses mutual "Transport Layer Security" (mTLS) to ensure communication is protected and encrypted between services, and sensitive user data is protected. It adds an extra layer of security without requiring additional encryption be added to each service manually. A service mesh can improve role-based access control (RBAC) and policies for securing APIs, and it can automate certificate management and key rotation.
- **Policy enforcement.** Service meshes include centralized configuration for service policies like quotas, rate-limiting, and authentication and authorization. It provides control over service interactions through access policies. Policies are enforced at the proxy level, which helps create consistency across services.
- **Traffic management.** Service mesh can help your apps manage traffic to individual services based on load conditions, versions, and user-specific rules. For example, if you're rolling out a new version of your inventory service, you can use a canary deployment to send only 5% of the traffic to the new service. (A canary is a smaller test deployment.) If that works, you can increase the traffic.
- **Health checks and observability.** It can be difficult to see the real-time interactions between microservices, but a service mesh allows you to use integrated observability technologies like

metrics collecting and distributed tracing. Sidecars in a service mesh collect metrics (request counts, latency, error rates) and send them to the control plane or monitoring tools.

- **Fault tolerance and increased resilience.** When microservices encounter failures, a service mesh can help by automating retries and fallbacks. If a service fails or becomes unresponsive, the service mesh will retry based on predefined rules and can reroute traffic to alternative services. This is to say that the app is able to cope with failure gracefully in the event that one of the services are unavailable to the user to achieve a good experience. Information on the delay of a successful retry is also collected by the service mesh. This data can be used to inform future regulations regarding the optimal wait time so that the system is not overloaded with unnecessary retries.

Development and operations teams are better prepared to manage the transition from monolithic systems to cloud-native apps—groups of tiny, autonomous, and loosely connected microservice applications—when they use a service mesh.

2.5.3 Challenges in Service Mesh Implementation

Organizations can experience challenges when implementing a service mesh, including:

- **Complexity and integration with existing systems.** A service mesh can be difficult to set up, manage, and integrate with existing systems. Organizations can encounter challenges if they are working in a large, distributed environment spanning multicloud and on-premises systems, or if they have not previously used a service mesh.
- **Resource requirements and operational overhead.** Service meshes can increase the operational overhead of managing applications because each service instance now has a sidecar proxy, which increases CPU and memory usage. Managing and troubleshooting, particularly in large-scale deployments, can be complex, and maintaining performance and scale can be more difficult as a result.

- **Skills gaps.** Teams need training to understand service mesh features, configuration, and best practices. Failure of debugging is serious and mostly when failure is caused by complicated routing rules or misconfigurations of mTLS. In numerous organizations, the current teams do not have the knowledge regarding the service mesh technology that might create a difficulty in the getting started and effective service mesh utilization.

2.5.4 Key Features of Integration Gateways

A cloud-managed service called Integration Gateway facilitates integrations between Insurance Suite and internal or external apps. Development teams design new integration projects, build them locally, then deploy them to Cloud Platform (GWCP) via the Integration Gateway's operations and architecture.

As a link between Insurance Suite and external applications, Integration Gateway is a crucial component of the Integration Framework. Usually, the Integration Gateway houses several integrations that use the Integration Framework technologies to communicate with Insurance Suite and other apps.

The process by which development teams create integrations is standardized and improved by Integration Gateway. The offered technologies guarantee that the developers have all the necessary components (languages, frameworks, libraries, and dependencies) to construct the application and that their software stack complies with operational requirements once the application is eventually put into production.

- To implement "Enterprise Integration Patterns" (EIP), Integration Gateway uses Apache Camel as the underlying integration framework. Design patterns are popular development strategies that have been shown to be successful for a particular issue. Developed design patterns and integration solutions for common system connection and data exchange issues, Camel is a Java-based implementation of EIP. With Apache Camel, you can use the REST "domain-specific language" (DSL) to develop REST services more quickly and easily.

- Integration Gateway is a versatile framework that facilitates the creation of cloud-native applications. Other features include building CI/CD pipelines, provisioning applications using Identity Federation Hub for authentication, and offering smooth integration for cloud deployment.
- The Integration Gateway offers independent scaling from Insurance Suite core apps with log analytics observability through the usage of microservices.
- The Gosu code in the Insurance Suite applications is removed when the integration functionality is moved to Integration Gateway.
- Because the integration apps operate independently of Insurance Suite, they may be developed and improved with no effect on Insurance Suite, improving flexibility and business agility.

Multiple Choice Questions (MCQs)

1. **What is the primary objective of an API-First strategy?**

   A. Building APIs after application development

   B. Designing APIs before implementing services

   C. Eliminating APIs from architecture

   D. Replacing databases with APIs

2. **Contract-Driven Design in APIs primarily focuses on:**

   A. Database schema design

   B. Predefined API specifications between providers and consumers

   C. Writing backend code first

   D. Developing UI components

3. **Which architecture enables systems to respond to events in real time?**

   A. Monolithic Architecture

   B. Layered Architecture

   C. Event-Driven Architecture

   D. Client-Server Architecture

4. **Which messaging system component ensures reliable communication between services in an event-driven platform?**

   A. Load Balancer

   B. Message Broker

   C. Firewall

   D. Cache Server

5. **Which API style uses HTTP methods such as GET, POST, PUT, and DELETE?**

   A. GraphQL

   B. REST

   C. gRPC

   D. SOAP

6. **Which API technology allows clients to request exactly the data they need in a single query?**

   A. REST

   B. GraphQL

   C. gRPC

   D. AsyncAPI

7. **gRPC primarily uses which protocol for communication?**
   A. HTTP/1.1
   B. HTTP/2
   C. FTP
   D. SMTP
8. **API versioning is mainly used to:**
   A. Improve UI performance
   B. Track changes in database systems
   C. Manage changes without breaking existing clients
   D. Reduce API documentation
9. **API governance ensures:**
   A. Faster hardware processing
   B. Standardization, security, and compliance in API usage
   C. Removal of documentation
   D. Replacement of integration tools
10. **What is the main purpose of a Service Mesh in microservices architecture?**
   A. Manage databases
   B. Handle service-to-service communication and observability
   C. Replace APIs
   D. Store application logs

Answers

1	2	3	4	5	6	7	8	9	10
B	B	C	B	B	B	B	C	B	B

3

Intelligent Platform Engineering

3.1 INTERNAL DEVELOPER PLATFORMS AND GOLDEN PATHS

The development team faces increased mental demands because contemporary cloud-native systems, microservice systems and DevOps automated infrastructure and distributed systems have become more complex (Adusumilli, 2025). Developers must now handle application logic development together with infrastructure provisioning and deployment pipeline management, observability tool implementation, security policy development, and compliance requirement fulfillment. The increase in operational demands led to the development of Internal Developer Platforms (IDP) which serve as structured solutions to simplify complex tasks while enhancing software delivery processes.

The Internal Developer Platform functions as a self-service platform that a dedicated platform engineering team creates and manages. Developers receive standard tools, workflow automation, reusable templates and infrastructure abstractions which enable them to create and launch applications. IDPs create an integrated development experience by unifying infrastructure elements, CI/CD pipelines, security controls and monitoring systems through a single interface which eliminates toolchain fragmentation.

One of the central ideas of internal developer platforms is that of Golden Paths. Golden paths are predefined workflows that outline the routine engineering operations of creating a new service, deploying an application, provisioning an infrastructure, or setting up observability. These tracks make the organization's best practices, governance standards, and security requirements repeatable processes. Instead of having teams recreating configurations, golden paths offer an effective and explicit path towards implementation of the normal development duties.

Internal Developer Platforms and Golden Paths are a move towards non-ad hoc DevOps practices in the direction of platform engineering. Organizations can use the developer experience as a product to maximize productivity, achieve compliance, and increase the operational resilience and speed with which software can be delivered at scale.

3.1.1 Foundations of Internal Developer Platforms

An Internal Developer Platform (IDP) refers to a self-service platform which has been developed and maintained by a platform engineering team within an organization to support application developers within the organization. It combines infrastructure, automation and deployment workflow, security controls with operational tooling into a single platform layer. Through the abstraction of repetitive and operational complexity, an IDP will allow developers to concentrate on providing business functionality, as well as keeping an eye on underlying systems.

Internal Customer Internal Developer Platforms are developed keeping internal customers (the developers) in mind. Platform teams are product-oriented where the IDP is perceived as a constantly changing internal product. The platform is developed iteratively through feedback loops and the roadmap in line with business goals to achieve the goal of satisfying engineering teams and operational consistency and governance.

One of the core notions of IDPs is the realization of golden paths, which are opinionated, standardized workflows, directing developers to complete such common tasks as the creation of services, provisioning of infrastructure, configuration of pipelines and deployment of applications. Organizational best practices, security needs and compliance requirements are captured in the form of golden paths and are integrated into the repeatable processes to minimize variability and enhance reliability across the teams.

Architecturally, an IDP is an orchestration and abstraction layer that is provided on top of existing enterprise tooling. It integrates various technologies into a harmonized system that will allow the self-service functionality and impose the governance by design. Internal Developer Platforms create the structural base of scalable, secure, and intelligent software delivery through standardization of workflows and automation into the development lifecycle.

3.1.2 Platform Engineering as a Product Discipline

Platform engineering is a software engineering field which is involved with the design, construction and maintenance of internal platforms, serving development teams. It was created based on the increasing complexity of modern cloud-native systems in which developers have to deal with infrastructure, automation, security, and operational tooling in addition to application logic. Platform engineering offers reusable and structured capabilities, which can be easily used to reduce this complexity and enhance productivity of the developer.

Platform engineering is characterized by the fact that the internal platforms are treated as products, and not as one-time infrastructure projects.

1. **Product-Oriented Mindset**

   Under product-oriented model, the Internal Developer Platform (IDP) is created and operated based on product management concepts.

   Platform teams:

   - Treat developers as internal customers
   - Define a clear product vision and roadmap
   - Conduct user research and gather feedback
   - Prioritize features based on developer needs
   - Continuously iterate and improve the platform

This attitude makes sure that the platform is developed in accordance with the business objectives and engineering needs.

2. **Developer Experience as a Core Objective**

   Platform engineering is deeply interested in enhancing developer experience (DevEx).

   Key goals include:

   - Reducing cognitive load
   - Standardizing workflows
   - Eliminating repetitive operational tasks
   - Enabling secure self-service capabilities
   - Improving time-to-market

   Platform engineering enhances delivery speed without jeopardizing the quality of work by streamlining developer operations and sacrificing high reliability and governance.

3. **Standardization and Governance by Design**

   In contrast to ad hoc DevOps automation, platform engineering incorporates governance as a capability of platforms.

   This includes:

   - Security policies encoded into workflows
   - Compliance requirements integrated into deployment pipelines
   - Infrastructure templates enforcing organizational standards
   - Automated guardrails to prevent misconfiguration

   When the platform is treated as a product, the controls are regularly implemented within teams.

4. **Continuous Improvement and Feedback Loops**

   Platform engineering emphasizes iterative evolution.

   Effective platform teams:

- Monitor platform usage metrics
- Collect structured feedback from developers
- Identify friction points in workflows
- Adapt the platform to emerging technologies
- Expand capabilities incrementally

This life cycle of continual improvement is what characterizes maturity of platform engineering practice over a fixed infrastructure management.

The product discipline of platform engineering is a strategic direction of enterprise software development. Having integrated engineering brilliance with product management concepts, organizations develop internal platforms, which grow in tandem with the business demands, increase developer output, and form sustainable basis of intelligent platform engineering.

3.1.3 Golden Paths: Standardized Development Workflows

An internal development platform (IDP) can facilitate a golden path, which is a predefined, paved road that offers developers an end-to-end process. A predetermined path guides developer to follow standard procedures which help them to work safely and maintain compliance with regulations. The golden path concept in software engineering is also known as the "happy path". Internal Developer Platforms (IDPs) use golden paths as fundamental elements of their systems.

A golden path is a planned, comprehensive process that leads developers through the usual routines, including provisions of the infrastructure, deployments of applications and configuration management. This model is created to remove the intricacies of the underlying infrastructure, giving the developers a chance to write code. It is anchored on standardization and automation that establishes uniform, repeatable procedures with the reduction of the possibility of human error and enhancement of operational efficiency.

The golden path's emphasis on self-service capabilities is among its most crucial elements. Without frequent communication with operations or infrastructure teams, the platform allows developers to operate autonomously to complete tasks. This style of self-service reduces wait times and development cycles.

But a golden path should not be understood as a strict limitation. As much as it gives an optimized route, it must permit the developers to divert when there is a need. It is aimed to give a supportive and effective means of work which allows innovativeness and consistency at the same time.

Why Golden Paths Matter

- **Reduced cognitive load:** Golden Paths frees developers to concentrate on developing code by abstracting away the complexity of deployments, infrastructure, and security setups.
- **Improved consistency and reliability:** Automated processes that are standardized carry out tasks in a uniform manner, reducing errors and boosting system dependability.
- **Faster development cycles:** Self-service features reduce project delays and allow developers to work more quickly.
- **Enhanced security and compliance:** Golden Paths protect operational operations while adhering to regulations by utilizing security best practices.

Examples of Golden Paths

- Configuring a database without worrying about the underlying setups by using a user interface or one of these code-based techniques.
- Providing a new service with established workflows and structures.
- Automated environment progression where a git push triggers automated policy checks and sign-offs.
- Spinning up ephemeral environments through automated workflows.
- Performing security sign-offs and policy checks as part of the deployment procedure.

3.1.4 Architectural Components of An Intelligent Developer Platform

An IDP tends to consist of the following components and features:

1. **Integration with existing tools and services**

   The integration ability of the platform enables the development teams to make use of their available investment in tools that facilitate version control, continuous integration and monitoring. It does not require a person to alternate the use of various tools and platforms, which results in a smooth workflow.

   The IDP can offer a flexible environment by integrating with a vast variety of tools and services. As an example, in a setup with Kubernetes as an orchestration tool, Jenkins as a CI/CD tool, and Prometheus as a monitoring tool, the platform can allow these separate tools to come together as one unified ecosystem.

2. **Application and infrastructure management**

   The IDP also provides a single point of control to maintain the application lifecycle and the foundational implementation that makes things easier to the developers and the ops teams. This involves provisioning resources, configuring networks, storage management, and scaling applications based on demand. Infrastructure experts are not required to deploy applications as developers do so.

   Infrastructure as code (IaC) is a feature of many IDPs, enabling teams to specify their infrastructure as code that can be versioned, reused, and shared. This strategy improves standardisation and reproducibility between environments, leading to a higher deployment speed, more reliable and more agile.

3. **Developer self-service capabilities**

   The platform allows the developers to do the work of provisioning environments, deploying applications, and accessing resources without being stranded by the operations teams. This minimizes bottlenecks and it provides the autonomy of team members.

Developers are able to test new ideas, iterate faster and introduce features at a lower rate.

The self-service features also facilitate better knowledge of the working side of software development. This would motivate developers to own their applications, which is in development up to production.

4. **Collaboration and governance**

   IDPs foster a participatory culture that promotes participative feedback, quicker feedback listening, and the solution of issues. It also contributes to governance through implementation of policies, standards and best practices throughout the lifecycle of development. This will guarantee this with security, regulatory and architectural needs.

   Governance capabilities in IDPs may involve role-based access control, auditing facilities, and automatic policy enforcement. All these features aid organizations to keep control over their development processes and infrastructure.

5. **Platform Orchestrator**

   An Intelligent Developer Platform centres around the platform orchestrator. The orchestrator is the control layer which links requests made by the developer to infrastructure, deployment pipelines, and governance policies. It comprehends configurations, uses predefined templates as well as coordinates provisioning, deployment and policy enforcement across settings.

   The orchestrator is combined with CI/CD systems, infrastructure tools, security controls as well as runtime environments to ensure workflows are performed in a consistent and automated fashion. The platform will minimize the need to have manual intervention by centralizing orchestration logic and potentially having standardized processes among teams.

6. **Developer Interface Layer**

   An Intelligent Developer Platform offers several interfaces where the developers can engage with the capabilities of the platform.

The interfaces can consist of a developer portal, command-line interface (CLI), APIs or code-based workload specifications.

The interface layer covers the complexity of the platform and still offers the accessibility to the underlying systems. With these interfaces, developers are able to provision resources, deploy services, get access to documentation and manage environment without necessarily knowing the specifics of infrastructure. This layer provides accessibility, usability and adoption between development teams.

7. **Observability and Monitoring**

   An Intelligent Developer Platform comprises of a vital architectural element observability. Monitoring, logging, and collection of metrics give a view on the application performance, health of the infrastructure and deployment status.

   Organizations can use observability to implement proactive detection of issues, expedite troubleshooting, and drive continuous improvement by integrating observability into the platform. In order to guarantee that the audit trail and performance data are preserved throughout the software lifecycle, governance and compliance are additionally supported by monitoring and feedback loops.

3.2 PLATFORM ENGINEERING FUNDAMENTALS AND VALUE STREAMS

The concept of platform engineering involves creating and managing internal platforms to enhance productivity and reliability of developer tasks and scalability of organizations. It uses product thinking to internal infrastructure where the platform is a product that the internal customers (developers) consume. It is aimed at minimizing cognitive load, workflow standardization, and self-service, as well as governance and security.

Fundamentally, platform engineering is about abstraction, automation and standardization. Platforms offer smooth roads, templates and autopilot functionality as opposed to developers mingling with complicated infrastructure. The solution is consistent to all teams and environments and quickens software delivery.

The value stream is one of the essential ideas of platform engineering. Value streams are the chain of processes that are needed to provide value to customers- idea to production. During these stream analysis and optimization, organizations are able to determine the bottlenecks, eliminate wastes as well as to enhance the efficiency of the flow. Platform engineering efforts usually start with mapping the software delivery value stream to identify where the friction points are and where platform capabilities might be used to produce measurable change.

Value stream thinking changes the emphasis on the technical optimizations which are remote to the optimization of the flow. Rather than optimizing on a single stage (e.g. CI/CD or provisioning), platform teams analyse the impact of changes on the whole lifecycle, such as development, testing, security reviews, deployment and operations. The complete assessment will demonstrate how platform investments produce measurable business outcomes which include reduced lead times and increased deployment rates and improved system reliability.

3.2.1 Core Principles of Platform Engineering

To achieve complete comprehension of platform engineering, all vital elements which create an effective internal developer platform need to be studied. The software delivery process benefits from these components which deliver better results through increased efficiency and improved security measures.

1. **Infrastructure Abstraction**

   Platform engineering operates as a core function to develop systems that enable developers to work without needing to access basic infrastructure elements. The system requires developers to write software through APIs and templates and automation scripts which enable them to use infrastructure resources without understanding complex system details. Platform engineers create systems which enable users to easily complete virtual machine provisioning and containerized application deployment and load balancer configuration tasks.

Examples of Abstraction in Infrastructure:

- **Cloud Infrastructure as Code (IaC):** Platform engineers may define and manage infrastructure using code with tools like Terraform and AWS CloudFormation, which facilitates the automation of cloud resource provisioning.
- **Kubernetes Abstractions:** To give developers a more straightforward interface for scaling apps, managing containers, and setting up network settings, platform engineers frequently layer on top of Kubernetes.

2. **Automation and Tooling**

The platform engineering field depends on automation as its fundamental principle. Through automation of their repetitive work, platform engineers provide developers with the ability to concentrate on coding while the platform manages all operational needs, which include system scaling, infrastructure provisioning, security enforcement, and performance monitoring. The automated system decreases human error risks while the development process achieves greater operational effectiveness.

Key Automation Tools:

- **CI/CD Pipelines**: Platforms can be integrated with CI/CD pipelines, which automate the processes of application development, testing, and deployment.
- **Configuration Management:** Platform engineers may automate the setup and administration of apps and infrastructure by using technologies like Ansible, Puppet, and Chef.
- **Monitoring and Alerts:** Prometheus and Grafana are examples of automated software that will make sure the platforms are operating continually and that an alert is delivered even in the event of a malfunction.

3. **Self-Service Platforms**

Engineers can perform their routine tasks through a functional internal system which enables them to work independently from operational support. The self-service system allows developers to implement their applications while they manage system configuration and performance monitoring without needing to understand the system's core infrastructure.

Benefits of Self-Service Platforms:

- **Increased Developer Autonomy:** Without having to wait for operations teams to provide them with the resources they require, developers may build new development environments, execute their code, and test their features.
- **Reduced Operational Bottlenecks:** Self-service platforms decrease operational demands which allows teams to concentrate on their essential strategic responsibilities.

4. **Security and Compliance**

The platform engineering process implements security and compliance requirements as foundational elements. Platform engineers must ensure that the platform complies with industry security requirements, such as SOC 2, HIPAA, and GDPR, as well as organizational security rules. They incorporate security controls into the platform's workflows, such as vulnerability detection, identity and access management (IAM), and encryption.

Key Security Practices:

- **Role-Based Access Control (RBAC):** The platforms implement strict access control measures, which allow only authorized users to access confidential information and conduct essential activities.
- **Encryption:** The system protects sensitive data through encryption methods, which secure data when it is stored and when it is transmitted.
- **Compliance Audits:** The platforms create audit logs, which security teams can examine to verify compliance with industry regulations and security standards.

5. **Value Streams and Flow Optimization**

   Platform engineering extends beyond its tool and infrastructure components because it exists to improve value delivery between the stages of ideation and production. A value stream is a complete path of activities that must be accomplished to provide software to customers. The process includes planning, development, testing, security review, and deployment, which together create operational procedures.

   Platform teams can use value stream analysis to identify delivery slowdowns, which result from bottlenecks, manual handoffs and repeated tasks. Platform engineering exists because organizations need to optimize their complete work systems instead of focusing on single tools and teams.

Key Aspects of Value Stream Alignment:

- **Lead Time Reduction:** The platform features such as automation, standard templates and self-service reduce the time delay between the time a code is committed and deployed.
- **Eradication of Bottlenecks:** Bottlenecks can be in form of manual approvals, delay of environment provisioning and security reviews that slows down delivery. These processes are incorporated in automated processes of platform engineering.
- **Flow Efficiency:** Organizations increase the rate of deployment and responsiveness to the needs of the business by reducing the waiting time and unnecessary handoffs.
- **Measurement and Feedback:** Metrics including deployment frequency, change failure rate, mean time to recovery (MTTR), and change lead time can be used to gauge the platform's impact on value streams.

3.2.2 Product Mindset and Developer Experience

Platform engineering views the internal platform as a product, and developers are the most important customers. In place of their exclusive focus on delivering infrastructure or tooling, platform teams are far more focused on delivering real developer solutions, improved workflows, and quantifiable outcomes. The platform is in a continuous development based on the user input, adoption, and the changing business needs.

The product mindset is not the same as a standard project-based one. Unlike delivering a fixed number of features and defaulting, platform teams operate on a long-term ownership, improvement and refinement of the platform takes place continuously to be useful, valuable and aligned to organizational goals. The implementation is also evaluated based on the satisfaction of the developers, the enhancement of the workflow, and the acceleration of delivery as well as the success of the implementation is also gauged on the technical implementation.

The most important part of this attitude is the Developer Experience (DevEx). Developer experience: This refers to the degree of effectiveness and efficiency with which developers can use the platform to complete tasks. An effective platform reduces the friction, eliminates manual workloads which is unnecessary and simplifies the routine processes such as environment provisioning, service deployment and configuration.

Key aspects of strong Developer Experience include:

- **Reduced friction:** Decreasing the number of contexts switches and also operational complexity in order to enable the developer write code.
- **Self-service enablement:** Allowing developers to self-provision resources and deploy apps without operations teams.
- **Clear interfaces and documentation:** Make them offer easy portal access, API and documentation that is easy to read and learn how the platform can be used.
- **Continuous feedback loops:** As a developer, the continuous feedback loops include gather feedback and usage data to make their platform improve.

Platform engineering can be used to help reduce the time-to-develop, enhance the adoption of platform capabilities, and improve alignment of the technical infrastructure to the business outcome through the integration of a product mindset with a strong emphasis on the developer experience.

3.2.3 Value Stream Mapping in Software Delivery

A lean management technique called value stream mapping (VSM) makes it easier to see how work moves from conception to production and spot bottlenecks and areas that need improvement. Organizations may better understand how work moves through their systems and pinpoint areas for waste reduction, productivity enhancement, and optimization for quicker and more dependable software delivery by outlining the value stream.

The entire value stream, from conception to delivery, may be seen via value stream mapping. VSM is used by physical industries to map the complete supply chain from raw materials to final products. Although knowledge labor entails converting concepts into experiences, records, and software, it nonetheless adheres to a step-by-step value generation process.

Flow is the constant, seamless movement of work through the value stream in software development and operations. When the operation proceeds smoothly, it suggests that there are few delays or obstacles, which reduces delivery time and efficiency. Another significant flow facilitator is continuous delivery (CD), which enables teams to produce software as frequently and reliably as possible by automating the software delivery process and establishing rapid feedback loops.

The benefits of VSM in terms of organization performance enhancement are immense:

- **Facilitates conversations:** Visual models of the value stream, workflow, and main metrics make it easier to talk and work with other team members. This understanding will enable the teams to engage in meaningful discussion regarding the software delivery process and this will help bring everyone on the same track relating to the shared objective of delivering software in a fast and reliable manner.
- **Identifies areas for improvement:** VSM Visualization Visualizing the software delivery process with the help of VSM allows visualizing the bottlenecks in the process and trace the effect of the improvement. VSM helps the teams to focus on the areas where they want to improve by identifying bottlenecks, waste, and inefficiencies.

- **Promotes continuous improvement:** By providing a framework for identifying and executing enhancements in a cyclical fashion, VSM and flow optimization support the culture of continuous improvement. Visualizations make it easier to monitor the effects of these enhancements and make necessary corrections.
- **Supports data-driven decision making:** Teams can make evidence-based decisions by using VSM's quantitative data on important indicators.
- **Documentation:** An essential component of the process is maintaining a precise, up-to-date record of the software development process. Making VSMs serves as a reminder of the path that has been travelled and aids in gaining a clear knowledge over time. A culture of continuous development requires confidence and morale, which may be developed by looking back and seeing progress over time.

Software delivery involves two essential value streams.

The first is the happy path, which is the standard delivery procedure used by teams to release updates and new features.

The "recovery value stream," or the process of recovering from an occurrence, is the second crucial value stream. This also entails the necessity of quickly deploying patches to production. These quick fixes are intended to reduce the risk and expense of downtime rather than adding value.

3.3 OBSERVABILITY, RELIABILITY, AND SELF-HEALING PLATFORMS

Contemporary software systems are highly distributed, cloud-native, and microservices-based in which complexity is the rule instead of the exception. The larger the scale of systems across regions, containers, API, and third-party services, the harder it becomes to comprehend the behavior of the systems. In this kind of settings, conventional methods of monitoring cannot work anymore. The platforms have to be designed in such a way that they offer deep visibility, quantifiable reliability and automated recovery.

Observability assists the teams in acquiring information about what is going on in the complex systems by collecting and analyzing the telemetry information that may comprise logs, metrics, and traces. Observability makes engineers be able to establish root causes of failures rather than detect failures to make informed or architectural decisions, improve prediction of future failures before they are not only observed but escalated. It substitutes the idea of reactive troubleshooting by the proactive knowledge of the systems.

Reliability on the other hand guarantees that systems will execute their intended functions under specified conditions. Performing platforms are more interested in reliability as an engineering practice that establishes measurable objectives and determines system performance with reference to these objectives. The idea of reliability in the contemporary platform engineering world is, in fact, not a coincidence, but a construction, and there are more approaches to the aspect of structured practices and feedback loops to enhance it and measure it.

Intelligent platforms are also self-healing in addition to being visible and reliable. The self-healing systems can automatically detect anomalies, isolate failures and take corrective measures. Automation will enable policy enforcement and resilience patterns, so the platforms can recover themselves within minutes after disruption, reduce downtimes and be able to go on with their offerings. Resilient and adaptive digital platforms are created with observability, reliability engineering and self-healing mechanisms.

3.3.1 Foundations of Observability: Logs, Metrics, and Traces

The capacity to measure a system's internal state using the data it produces—typically in the form of logs, metrics, and traces—is known as observability. It gives teams the ability to recognize, look into, and resolve issues in intricate, dispersed settings.

Observability in DevOps and cloud-native systems extends beyond monitoring to offer some background knowledge of why a system is acting in a particular manner and not merely that something has broken. Logs are event records, metrics are quantifiable data with time, and traces display how requests move through services.

The issue of observability is a cross-cutting issue that cabs across all code or infrastructure. This does not imply that it should be able to get into the business logic or influence infrastructure architecture. However, it needs to act as an all-perceiving, omnipresent eye that is "spying" on your distributed architecture in real time. In a subsequent section, we will examine the practical implementation of this.

As an approach, observability relies on three pillars: logs, metrics, and traces. Each pillar is crucial in providing organizations with the necessary visibility about their system and how to enhance it.

1. **Logs**

   Logs are documentation of network or application events. They record system conditions, errors, and activity. Logs are valuable for troubleshooting, analyzing, and monitoring a system's health and performance.

   Typically, machine-generated data from routers, databases, apps, and other components makes up a log file. It is generated automatically in response to system configurations, logins, problems, and other events.

   Logs are essential for diagnosing problems and comprehending system activity. They contain a range of relevant information, including:

   - Timestamps
   - User ID or IP Address
   - Transaction ID
   - Details About an Event or Error

   Logs, as a foundation of observability, offer improved insight into a system's health and performance. To make it simple for DevOps and platform teams to find behavioral patterns, fix problems, and extract actionable insights, log entries are categorized in a system.

2. **Metrics**

   Metrics are collections of numerical data used to evaluate and examine several facets of a system, such as its behavior, performance, or features. To maximize performance, they support the understanding of patterns, the detection of abnormalities, and the making of well-informed decisions.

Metrics are usually obtained by keeping an eye on particular system parameters. By gathering metrics or key performance indicators (KPIs), you can obtain the following data, depending on how they are configured:

- CPU Usage
- Memory Utilization
- Error Rates
- Network Latency
- Response Time

A crucial element of observability is metrics. They provide the quantitative information required to comprehend and improve a network's or system's performance.

Teams may efficiently control and improve their systems by using observability platforms, which process measurements in real-time (or almost real-time). These technologies provide comprehensive insights and encourage proactive problem-solving to ensure network or application performance.

3. **Traces**

The recordings of a request's or transaction's execution path as it passes through a system are called traces. Along with the amount of time spent at each step, they provide a comprehensive chronological explanation of the components and services the request interacts with.

The "instrumentation of code" in the system creates observability traces. Events and timestamps may be included as requests move through the system. Once they were sewn together, the traces included the path history of every request.

Information found in traces can be used to troubleshoot and improve a system's performance. Among these data are:

- Duration of Operations
- Sequences of Services
- Root Cause of Errors
- Path of Requests

Traces, one of the foundations of observability, allow you to familiarize yourself with the intricacy of your system. It provides a comprehensive picture of how requests behave, making troubleshooting and request optimization easier. In other words, it provides a visual map of the requests.

3.3.2 Engineering for Reliability: SLOs, SLIs, and Error Budgets

Reliability engineering concepts, which are vital in ensuring that teams measure, manage and balance the performance and stability of the system, are SLIs, SLOs, and Error Budgets. Whereas observability offers an understanding of system behavior, these reliability mechanisms establish quantifiable benchmarks on which systems can be confident to deliver customer expectations without necessarily eliminating the possibility of innovation.

A **Service Level Indicator (SLI)** is a particular measure to quantify an element of the degree of service delivery to customers. Reliability is measured by SLIs using metrics like uptime, latency, error rate, or response time which can be measured. They are generally given in terms of percentages with 100 percent being the level of perfection. Defining of reliability objectives is based on SLI.

A **Service Level Objective (SLO)** is a performance goal that is set within an organization based on one or more SLIs. It defines the required degree of dependability in a specific time. As an example, a streaming service can have an SLO of 99.9% uptime per month. It implies that the service can fail not more than 43.2 minutes once a month. SLOs can be used to transform customer expectations into quantifiable engineering objectives and establish responsibility within teams before failure can happen into incidents that are visible to the customer.

An **Error Budget** is the acceptable level of failure within a specific time frame and at the same time fulfilling the SLO. The error budget is the allowable margin of error of either downtime or degraded performances since no system can have the 100 percent reliability. An example would be in the event that the SLO is 99.9% availability, the remaining 0.1 is the error budget that can be tolerated.

Error budgets allow a viable tradeoff between innovation and stability. When the error budget is not used significantly, teams can be certain about whether to release new features and experiment. When the budget runs out, then there is a shift in emphasis to reliability enhancement and risk reduction. This mechanism is such that engineering velocity does not affect the stability of the systems.

A combination of SLIs, SLOs, and error budgets offer a systematic approach to the creation of credible systems. They help balance technical performance and business expectations and allow the teams to take more data-driven decisions regarding risk, the frequency of deployment, and operation priorities.

3.3.3 Self-Healing and Autonomous Platform Operations

Self-healing systems are developed to automatically detect, diagnose and fix failures. The manual recovery of the modern distributed systems is too slow and inaccurate. Self-healing mechanisms are made up of continuous monitoring, smart detection and automated response that make sure that systems are available and stable.

1. **Self-Healing Systems**

   Self-healing systems are automated systems which are developed in order to detect, analyze and solve issues automatically. These systems routinely check themselves and their performance, attract problems or potential failures and take corrective action in an effort to reach optimal functionality.

   It is self-healing infrastructure rather than raising alarms and letting engineers correct them, which brings an infrastructure to a healthy state in real time, which only needs a lesser dependency on manual management and improved availability of systems.

2. **Core Capabilities of Self-Healing Platforms**

   Self-healing systems combine:

   - Continuous observability
   - Intelligent failure detection
   - Automated decision-making
   - Real-time remediation

   They allow improving the root-cause identification and automatic recovery by linking telemetry signals through distributed settings.

3. **AI-Driven and Autonomous Operations**

   Sophisticated self-healing mechanisms rely on machine learning and artificial intelligence to identify abnormalities, determine reasons and automatically implement remedies. Such systems may become better with time and forecast, avoid and fix the problem without human efforts.

   Independent operation automatically shifts response to resilience of platforms in an incident.

4. **Self-Healing in Practice: Cloud-Native Platforms**

   - Modern cloud-native platforms incorporate built-in self-healing capabilities. For example:
   - Failed containers can be automatically restarted
   - Unhealthy workloads can be rescheduled
   - Desired state can be continuously enforced

   The platforms such as Kubernetes support the health and availability of workloads by keeping the system converged to its desired state as per its definition.

3.4 INFRASTRUCTURE AS CODE AND ENVIRONMENT AUTOMATION

The contemporary platform engineering requires extensive automation to promote consistency, scalability, and reliability across the environments.

With the increase in the complexity and dispersion of systems, infrastructure provisioning or environment configuration is inefficient, prone to errors and unsustainable manually. Infrastructure as Code (IaC) provides a solution to this dilemma since it allows teams to represent infrastructure in declarative or programmatic form, and can be versioned, tested and deployed like application code.

Infrastructure as Code is the concept that changes infrastructure management into an automated and repeatable engineering practice, as opposed to a manual operational activity. Rather than making ad-hoc script configuration or hand-made changes to consoles, infrastructure definitions are defined in source control systems and reviewed using pull requests and deployed using automated pipelines. This will enhance traceability as well as minimize configuration drift and provide a consistent environment between development, staging, and manufacturing.

Environment automation builds on these principles with the provisioning, configuration, scaling and lifecycle management of environments being automated. Whether it is spinning up temporary testing environments, or pushing workloads across many stages, automation has been able to keep infrastructure and apps aligned dynamically and predictably to application needs. This allows it to develop faster, increase reliability, and reduce operation overhead.

Environment automation and Infrastructure as Code make up a lower level of intelligent platform engineering. They facilitate reproducibility, provide standardization, facilitate compliance, and offer the flexibility needed by the current cloud-native systems.

3.4.1 Principles and Models of Infrastructure as Code

Infrastructure as Code (IaC) is a methodology where infrastructure configurations and provisioning are defined and managed using code rather than manual processes. This approach treats infrastructure like software, allowing teams to write, test, and deploy infrastructure configurations in a controlled and repeatable manner.

IaC eliminates the need for manual infrastructure setup, which often leads to inconsistencies and inefficiencies. By adopting IaC, organizations can ensure that their infrastructure is version-controlled, easily reproducible, and aligned with best practices for DevOps automation.

Importance of Infrastructure as Code in DevOps

IaC is an important part of DevOps processes, as it allows to automate the work smoothly, control the version, and quickly deploy something. Here's why it is important:

- **Consistency and Standardization:** IaC helps to provide consistency to the configurations of environments hence there is less variance between production, testing, and development environments.
- **Automation and Efficiency:** Automates the provisioning of infrastructure, eliminating human error and saving time.
- **Scalability:** Supports large-scale infrastructure management, enabling faster scaling up or down as per business requirements.
- **Cost Reduction:** Minimizes resource wastage by ensuring optimal allocation and usage.
- **Version Control and Reproducibility:** Enables tracking of changes, rollback mechanisms, and reproducibility across environments.

Key Principles of Infrastructure as Code

- **Idempotency:** Ensures that applying the same infrastructure script multiple times results in the same state without unintended side effects.
- **Modularization:** Encourages reusability of infrastructure components to simplify maintenance and updates.
- **Version Control:** Infrastructure code should be stored in Git, GitHub, GitLab, or Bitbucket to enable tracking, auditing, and rollback.
- **Security and Compliance:** Enforces security policies, access control, and compliance requirements through code.

There are 2 approaches to IaC:

Declarative approach: In a declarative approach to IaC, an IaC tool will setup the system for you by defining the intended state, including the resources you require and any qualities they should have.

Additionally, a declarative approach maintains a record of your system objects' present states, which facilitates the management of infrastructure removal.

Imperative method: In an IaC imperative approach, the precise commands required to accomplish the intended configuration are specified. Then, those directions must be carried out in the proper sequence.

Declarative in nature, many IaC tools offer the needed infrastructure automatically. Declarative IaC tools apply changes you make to the intended state for you, while imperative tools need you to choose how those changes should be applied.

Although IaC tools can function in both ways, they typically favor one over the other.

3.4.2 Infrastructure Provisioning and Configuration Management

1. **Infrastructure Provisioning**

   The process of designing and distributing IT infrastructure (including virtual servers, storage systems, network elements, and services controlled by clouds) is known as infrastructure provisioning. Its main goal is to have the underlying infrastructures that are needed to accommodate applications and workloads.

   Provisioning tools do code definition and maintain the infrastructure in the desired state. They are able to author, modify or regenerate resources on a demand basis which allows reproducibility and uniformity across environments.

   Provisioning usually comes before configuration and deployment proceedings.

2. **Configuration Management**

   Configuration management involves the process of configuration of provisioned infrastructure resources. This involves installing necessary software, system setups, system security policy applications and ensuring that there is consistency across settings of various environments.

   Configuration management tools are idempotent meaning that the same configuration should have the same system state with repeated application without any side effects that were not originally intended.

   Configuration drift is also handled using these tools. In case a system has some manual changes, some configuration management mechanisms take the system back to the desired state as defined.

Infrastructure Provisioning vs Configuration Management

The provisioning of infrastructure and configuration management are complementary and different:

- Provisioning comes up with infrastructure resources like networks and servers.
- Configuration management deploys and configures applications in the provisioned resources.
- Infrastructure layer is defined by provisioning.
- Configuration management identifies the application and system configuration layer.

Combined, these practices can provide the total lifecycle automation of the environments of infrastructure and Applications.

3.4.3 Environment Automation and Lifecycle Management

Automation of the environment Automation of the environment is the process of using tools and pre-written scripts to automatically provision, configure, update and operate software environments throughout the software delivery lifecycle - development to production - with no human intervention. It is one of the major components of contemporary DevOps, as it allows the teams to react fast to the changes, minimize the errors, and enhance the level of consistency in various environments. Automation reduces human effort and enhances consistency, in that, it standardizes the environment setup and minimizes human-related inconsistency.

The Benefits of Environment Automation

- **Faster Deliveries:** Organizations can cut dramatically the amount of time between code commit and production deployment by automating repetitive tasks such as environment creation, configuration and testing.
- **Consistency Across Environments:** Scripts and templates are automated, which makes the development, testing, staging, and production environments consistent and minimizes the deployment failures due to differences in environments.
- **Scalability:** Automated workflows dynamically provide a high or low environment based on demand with no manual intervention and can allow teams to effectively support large distributed systems.
- **Operational Efficiency:** Automation enables infrastructure and operations departments to concentrate on more valuable work through removing the repetitive manual work.

Environment Automation in the DevOps Lifecycle

The automation of the environment is found as a part of the wider DevOps cycle, which focuses on the processes of continuous integration, delivery, and deployment. Modern DevOps workflows use automation tools to:

- Automatically provision development environments when a feature branch is created.
- Trigger environment setup as part of CI/CD pipelines.
- Recreate test or staging environments on demand.
- Push fully configured environments into production with minimal human input.

This integration will guarantee that all changes go through the same automated lifecycle, and that the quality of an idea to production is consistent and of high quality.

Lifecycle Management Through Automation

Lifecycle management is the continuous process of managing and developing environments during their lifespan:

- **Creation:** The environments are created by automated scripts using configuration templates.
- **Testing and Validation:** Environments are automatically validated via automated tests as part of a CI pipeline.
- **Promotion:** Automated workflows can be used to promote environments between development stages and staging and production.
- **Scaling and Adjustment:** Environments are scaled in response to performance needs or operational load.
- **Termination and Clean-up:** As such, environments that are not in use or have emerged obsolete are automatically de-provisioned, saving resources and thereby saving the associated costs.

The combination of environment automation with lifecycle management enables organizations to create their required business environments which remain stable throughout the software delivery process.

3.4.4 Governance, Compliance and Policy as Code

Governance as code is the art of expressing, implementing and verifying organizational policies in executable and machine-readable code, as opposed to manual documentation. It makes sure that there is autonomy in the rules that are applied wherever infrastructure and services are implemented.

Practically, governance as code builds upon infrastructure as code by codifying policies regarding security, access control, cost limits, and compliance. Whereas infrastructure as code deals with provisioning resources, governance as code consists of the manner in which these resources should act and what restrictions they need to be bound by.

The introduction of the cloud is flexible and complex. In the absence of governance, teams either exceed their resources provision, break budgets or leave their systems vulnerable. Governance as code fills that gap between what you have already decided to do and what actually gets implemented.

Typical policies cover these areas:

- **Security controls:** Requirements for encryption, who can access what, and how networks should be configured
- **Cost management:** Limits on resources, tags that track budgets, and spending caps
- **Compliance requirements:** Automated enforcement of regulations like GDPR, HIPAA, or SOC 2
- **Operational standards:** Naming conventions, configuration patterns, and deployment best practices

Manual governance breaks at cloud scale. As your infrastructure grows, keeping track of who can do what, ensuring compliance, and preventing misconfigurations becomes overwhelming.

- **Deployment speed:** Automated policy checks enable teams to deploy quickly while remaining compliant.
- **Consistency everywhere:** When policies exist as code, they apply the same way in development, staging, and production.
- **Audit readiness:** Every policy decision is logged with context.
- **Scalability:** Governance as code works the same whether you're managing ten resources or 10,000.

Compliance as code

Compliance as Code is how companies handle and automate rules they need to follow using code. By turning compliance rules into code, companies ensure they stick to the rules all the time, reduce mistakes people might make, and boost their overall safety.

- Consistency: Automating compliance influences all environments by sticking to the same standards and reducing differences.
- Auditability: Automated compliance gives a clear, documented trail of following rules.
- Scalability: IaC allows compliance practices to scale across big and complex infrastructures.
- Error Reduction: It reduces human mistakes, ensuring compliance rules are always followed.

Policy as Code

In this context, a policy is any type of rule, condition, or instruction that governs IT operations or processes.

Policy-as-code is the use of code to define and manage rules and conditions. Under a policy-as-code approach, teams write out policies using some type of programming language, such as Python, YAML, or Rego.

When engineers need to make updates, they do so by modifying the existing code. They can also share the code with others using version control systems (VCS). They can use a policy-as-code enforcement engine to ensure policies are met.

- **Efficiency:** Policies can be shared and enforced automatically at scale.
- **Speed:** The ability to automate policy enforcement results in faster operations than a manual approach.
- **Visibility:** When policies are defined in code, stakeholders can review which code-based policies are in place.
- **Collaboration:** Policy-as-code simplifies collaboration between developers, security, and operations teams.
- **Accuracy:** Teams avoid the risk of making configuration mistakes when managing a system manually.
- **Version control:** Policy-as-code ensures that you can revert to an earlier configuration if needed.

- **Testing and validation:** Policies written in code can be validated using automated auditing tools.

3.5 DEVELOPER EXPERIENCE AND PRODUCTIVITY ENGINEERING

Infrastructure, automation and scalability are not the only concerns that modern software delivery is all about, but also about the experience of the creators of systems and their operation. With the organizations switching to cloud-native architecture, microservice, and platform engineering, the complexity of the development ecosystem grows substantially. To cope with this complexity and continue to be fast and quality-based, it is essential to pay much attention to Developer Experience (DevEx).

Developer Experience: The experience includes the way developers perceive and engage with the tools and processes, the platforms and workflows offered by the organization. It includes onboarding and documentation processes, CI/CD pipelines, infrastructure access, observability tools, and internal platforms. Good developer experience will lessen the friction, fast-track delivery, and enhance the engineering performance.

Productivity Engineering builds on this concept by developing a systematic way of measuring, optimizing and enhancing systems that facilitate developers to create value. Rather than looking at output measures like line of code, or number of features, productivity engineering reduces itself to flow efficiency, cognitive load, and frequency of deployments, reliability and patterns of collaboration.

Companies who have invested in developer experience and productivity engineering always realize shorter release timeframes, better software quality, increased developer satisfaction and better business results. One of the key benefits in platform-based modern environments is developer experience as a strategic priority and not a secondary one.

3.5.1 Foundations of Developer Experience (DevEx)

Developer experience (DevEx) refers to the technology, processes and culture that define software development in an organization. It describes how well an engineering culture incentivizes quality work, and how easy it is to get things done.

Developer experience comprises all activities that development teams must partake in as part of their role in the software development process. It's an umbrella term covering developers' multiple daily activities and can include removing the bottlenecks identified above or proactively enabling developers through DevOps.

A good developer experience is a measure of how empowered your developers are to complete the tasks that help the team move forward quickly on the project. The speed at which your developers produce quality work is an important metric in the software development process, and enhancing developer experience is one way to increase their speed. By enabling developers to do their best work without unnecessary burdens, you can simultaneously improve their efficiency and happiness.

For instance, how easily can a new developer spin up a microservice and set up their local environment? Do they need to spend an entire week wiring the hardware and looking at documentation? Or is there already a script they can run that will have all necessary configurations built for them? Other considerations include the time it takes to develop software locally and how complicated it is to set up some examples. If a local microservice environment already exists, can a developer simply wire in a new service and test it without doing mocks?

Infrastructure provisioning is another component of the developer's job. The infrastructure being based on TerraForm or AWS can change the developer's workflow. For infrastructure based on AWS, developers might need to contact people with access to the AWS console who are willing to help out. The ease with which a developer can start using new technologies is an important aspect of the developer experience.

Importance of Developer Experience

There are many tangible reasons why DevEx drives innovation and stability and increases productivity and output. A considerable majority of respondents to Forrester's Opportunity Snapshot believe that improved DevEx can drive productivity (74%), shorten time to market (77%) and increase customer satisfaction (85%).

But there is a host of intangibles to best practice DevEx too. Productive, happy colleagues are better to be around, and an overall sense of pride and alignment with the company's mission is a rising tide that lifts all boats.

Let's further examine the role that DevEx plays in your developers' work life and its contribution to the software development process. It can significantly improve the following:

- **Developer Productivity**: By improving working conditions and enabling developers to take more pride in their work, DevEx enables developer to perform their roles with more ease and efficiency. A positive developer experience streamlines workflows, reduces friction, and allows developers to focus on writing high-quality code, ultimately leading to faster development cycles and improved productivity. It's even possible to track these improvements in developer productivity, although it's important to remember that DevEx and developer productivity are not the same thing.
- **Attracting and Retaining Talent**: Building a reputation for a stimulating and engaging working environment allows you to attract and retain top talent in the competitive tech industry. When developers are willing and able to do their best and there is high morale and less churn in the engineering team. By providing the right tools, support, and a conducive work environment, developers can become advocates for their employers and help with retention and recruitment.
- **Innovation and Creativity**: Innovation is just another word for solving problems, and good DevEx involves creating an environment for doing creative work and focusing your time on hard problems. An environment that encourages deep work represents good DevEx and the ideal platform for innovation.
- **Competitive Advantage**: If you're innovating, attracting the top talent and enabling them to do their best work, competitive advantage will follow from this. Developers are arguably the most important resource at your disposal, and using them correctly can be a competitive advantage of its own.

- **Customer Satisfaction**: Customers want high-quality, reliable products and serviced delivered on deadline. Software companies that prioritize DevEx create the environment needed for developer to deliver these, and enjoy their work while doing so. A positive developer experience contributes to the creation of stable, feature-rich applications, ultimately enhancing the end-user experience and satisfaction with the delivered products.

All of the above helps to reduce costs, improving the bottom line. The Developer Experience Lab also has more on the tangible benefits of DevEx improvements.

3.5.2 Reducing Cognitive Load And Improving Developer Flow

Cognitive load is the mental effort the developers have to put in order to accomplish a task. The mental energy of developers is used in overheads rather than to address actual issues when cognitive load is high, consuming productivity and frustrating them. Cognitive load reduction involves providing clarity by way of endorsed documentation, tooling uniformity, visible procedures, and code organization, narrative, and organization.

To explain the concept of the mental effort, the theory of cognitive load is used; the mental efforts may be divided into two types: intrinsic load (the complexity of the task) and extraneous load (distracters that are irrelevant to the task and are created by inefficient ways). Cognitive load is also used in software engineering to define the mental stress a software engineer has to go through to accomplish a task such as being familiar with codebase, dependencies, and workflows. The working memory of a developer can be overloaded by the amount of details he or she has to remember, contributing to a higher number of errors, lower creativity, and slower work.

Poor tool integration, fragmented tooling, slow builds, high context switching, manual processes and inconsistent automation are some examples of process friction that introduce irrelevant burden on developers. These inefficiencies do not only slow down the delivery process, they also disrupt flow-states the times during which people are in deep, negative concentration and most productive and successful in solving problems.

Cognitive burden can be greatly reduced through streamlining deployment processes, reducing manual interventions and offering clear and easily available documentation. Avoiding causes of friction enables developers to be focused and devote more time useful work.

Organizations can facilitate better productivity of the developers, minimize errors, enhance a smooth flow in their work processes, and enhance the overall experience of the developers, by reducing cognitive load, and friction of the processes involved in the work.

3.5.3 Measuring and Engineering Productivity

To measure the productivity and flow of developers, it is important to track metrics which measure the effectiveness and efficiency of the software development processes but not to be simplistic with output measures. The classic measures of productivity used, e.g. lines of code or number of tickets, are not able to show the whole picture of value flow within an engineering organization and may be deceptive when taken in isolation. Modern metrics of productivity integrate delivery and quality metrics and developer experience metrics to make measurements of engineering performance consistent.

One widely used framework for measuring engineering performance is the DORA metrics, which include:

- **Lead time for changes** – the time between committing code and deploying it to production.
- **Deployment frequency** – how often teams successfully push changes to production.
- **Change failure rate** – the percentage of deployments that cause production failures.
- **Time to restore service** – how long it takes to recover from a failure in production.

Monitoring these metrics enables the teams to understand the pace, stability, and quality with which they deliver products, as well as to detect the bottlenecks and ineffective steps in the development pipeline.

Other flow measures besides DORA measures include cycle time (the duration of time taken between the commencement of work and its completion) and work in progress can be used to determine how well work flows through the development process, enabling teams to know where it gets stuck.

The effective measurements also think about more general productivity indicators, which include team collaboration and user satisfaction with release and developer experience indicators. Productivity exists as a system-level result which depends on multiple results from individual components.

Organizations can use these metrics to measure their engineering productivity, which they can then analyze and optimize for development performance that needs to match business value while achieving ongoing improvements.

Multiple Choice Questions (MCQs)

1. **What is the primary purpose of an Internal Developer Platform (IDP)?**

   A. To replace developers in software development

   B. To provide standardized tools and workflows for developers

   C. To eliminate the need for infrastructure

   D. To reduce the number of applications

2. **In platform engineering, "Golden Paths" refer to:**

   A. The most profitable business process

   B. The standard and recommended way to build and deploy software

   C. The security policies used in organizations

   D. The testing framework used by developers

3. **Which concept focuses on mapping how value is delivered through software development processes?**

   A. Value Streams

   B. Data Pipelines

   C. Network Streams

   D. Testing Cycles

4. **Which of the following is a core objective of Platform Engineering?**

   A. Increase manual infrastructure management

   B. Reduce developer productivity

   C. Enable faster and reliable software delivery

   D. Eliminate automation tools

5. **Which practice involves monitoring systems through logs, metrics, and traces?**

   A. Automation

   B. Observability

   C. Integration

   D. Virtualization

6. **A self-healing platform is designed to:**

   A. Automatically detect and recover from failures

   B. Replace all IT staff

   C. Eliminate the need for monitoring

   D. Prevent all software bugs

7. **Which technology practice allows infrastructure to be defined and managed using code?**

   A. Continuous Integration

   B. Infrastructure as Code (IaC)

   C. Agile Development

   D. Microservices Architecture

8. **Which benefit is associated with environment automation?**

   A. Manual server configuration

   B. Faster and consistent environment setup

   C. Increased configuration errors

   D. Reduced scalability

9. **Developer Experience (DevEx) primarily focuses on:**

   A. Increasing infrastructure cost

   B. Improving tools, workflows, and productivity for developers

   C. Limiting developer access to systems

   D. Reducing software releases

10. **Which factor most directly improves developer productivity engineering?**

    A. Complex workflows

    B. Manual deployments

    C. Streamlined tooling and automation

    D. Reduced collaboration

Answers

1	2	3	4	5	6	7	8	9	10
B	B	A	C	B	A	B	B	B	C

4

Cloud-Native Integration and Distributed System

4.1 KUBERNETES-BASED INTEGRATION PLATFORMS

The modern cloud-native architecture requires scalable, resilient, portable and automation-friendly integration platforms. Traditional middleware systems were developed to operate in a static environment usually in fixed virtual machines or dedicated hardware. Nonetheless, distributed systems that use hybrid and multi-cloud environments need a more dynamic and coordinated framework (Lin and Macvittie, 2022). It is here that the integration platforms which are Kubernetes-based have become a revolutionary platform.

Kubernetes has now become more than a container orchestrating system and is a building block of a cloud-native infrastructure. Kubernetes offers a homogeneous setting of deploying, scaling, and managing integration services by abstracting computer, networking, and storage resources. The integration workloads of API gateways, message brokers, service meshes, and data pipelines are now achievable in Kubernetes-orchestrated containerized microservices.

Kube Based integration platform allows enterprises to decouple integration logic and infrastructure dependencies. Organizations no longer have tightly integrated middleware stacks but instead deploy loosely integrated, composition-contained units of integration that can be automatically scaled as demand surges. The strategy enhances fault tolerance, rolling updates, observability, and aligns integration strategy with DevOps and Gitops process flows.

Kubernetes gives the operational foundation to the latest integration architectures as distributed systems are increasingly event-driven and API-centric. It helps achieve declarative setup, infrastructure as code, automatic healing, and high scalability so that it is a perfect runtime to high-scale enterprise integration platforms.

4.1.1 Containerized Middleware and Microservices Integration

Cloud computing, particularly cloud-native computing, has changed from being monolithic to being microservices based. The way programs are created, implemented, and run has changed as a result of this change. These days, cloud-native apps are thought to be the foundation of the contemporary digital economy , running in large-scale cloud data centres and supporting distributed systems across industries.

An application is divided into several services by the microservices architecture, each of which is in charge of a certain task. Building cloud-native apps with microservices—especially containerised microservices—has emerged as a popular architectural strategy. Within containers like Docker containers, every microservice is bundled with all of its dependencies, libraries, and runtime modules. When called upon, these cloud-deployed containers carry out their respective functions.

The middleware is important in facilitating communication and coordination between distributed microservices. The secure login services, user interfaces, databases, machine learning services, and communication layers based on API are independent services, yet they should communicate with each other smoothly. Containerization also provides consistency of deployments in different environments and also provides APIs to enable core functionality between services.

Nevertheless, it is not enough to microservice-ify. Such containers are to be handled with the help of a container orchestration system like Kubernetes (K8s). Kubernetes simplifies cluster computing, operations management, networking, governance, resource efficiency, workload consolidation, and deployment. It has become the de facto container orchestration tool used to manage containers in production environments worldwide.

To orchestrate Microservices that are containerized, Kubernetes Deployments are created for each service to manage the desired state and enable scaling. Kubernetes Services expose microservices internally or externally, enabling communication and load balancing. Inter-service communication is configured using environment variables, ConfigMaps, and service endpoints. To ensure performance across a range of workloads, "Horizontal Pod Autoscaling" (HPA) dynamically scales the number of instances based on resource utilization.

Configuration management is handled using ConfigMaps and Secrets to separate application logic from configuration and sensitive data. Ingress controllers manage external access and routing to microservices. Deployment strategies such as rolling updates ensure seamless updates without downtime. Integration with CI/CD pipelines enables Continuous deployment of containerized microservices, continuous integration, and automated testing.

Through containerization and orchestration, middleware and microservices integration becomes scalable, resilient, and operationally efficient, forming a foundational layer for distributed cloud-native systems.

4.1.2 Service Mesh and API Gateway Orchestration

An API gateway is software that sits in front of a group of application programming interfaces (APIs). It routes API calls (also known as API requests) to the appropriate API and manages the delivery of data and services from the API back to API consumers (also known as API clients).

For API calls, the API gateway serves as a single point of entry. It acts as a control center for API call and response traffic. It does not matter if the APIs are hosted on-premises, in the cloud, or at a separate corporate entity. API calls can similarly come to the API gateway from various sources. API gateways are usually part of a broader API management and security solution that handles API discovery, API security, policy enforcement, and related capabilities. They can also balance traffic between API instances and handle load balancing, failover, and other issues related to API reliability and availability.

A service mesh is a technology pattern that takes the form of an infrastructure layer that operates on top of microservices. A service mesh handles communication between microservices. It routes messages back and forth while securing the data in the process. Working in this way, a service mesh facilitates observability, reliability, and security for the microservices in the architecture. In large-scale microservices architectures, a service mesh helps manage multiple services and ensures the reliability and availability the application requires.

Authentication and traffic management in API gateways and service meshes

Both API gateways and services mesh play crucial roles in traffic management and authentication. A service mesh will control internal traffic between microservices, with APIs, whereas an API gateway will include authentication to restrict access to particular APIs to authorized users and will distribute requests appropriately and safely. The service mesh can manage traffic, including granular control, e.g. load balancing within microservices, and rerouting traffic in the face of service failures. These technologies are critical in a cloud-native environment, where scaling and reliability are critical.

Both technologies handle requests and responses, routing data across networks, and can support service discovery and policy enforcement such as rate limiting and access controls. However, their primary focus differs. A service mesh is designed to manage microservice-to-microservice interactions, whereas an API gateway manages traffic between external clients and APIs.

A commonly used conceptual distinction is that an API gateway handles "north-south" traffic, which originates from outside the network and flows inward and outward, while a service mesh manages "east-west" traffic, meaning internal communication between microservices. Although this distinction is useful for understanding their roles, it is not absolute in all implementations.

4.1.3 Event-Driven Messaging and Streaming on Kubernetes

The importance of streaming and event-driven messaging as an architectural pattern of cloud-native systems is essential. In an event-driven architecture, services emit events on state changes and receive them at their own pace. The model is especially well-suited to distributed microservices settings on Kubernetes, where high uptime, scalability, and availability are key factors.

A distributed system must have a reliable, high-throughput communication system to distribute data among services. It is offered by event streaming platforms built on top of Kubernetes that enable the provision of persistent, fault-tolerant, and scalable delivery of messages between clusters.

Event-Driven Architecture in Cloud-Native Systems

In an event-driven model:

- Producers generate events when actions or state changes occur.
- Events are transmitted through a messaging or streaming platform.
- Consumers subscribe to relevant events and react independently.

The decoupling allows the producers and consumers not to have any awareness of one another, enhancing system flexibility and making services deployment and scaling independent.

Streaming Platforms on Kubernetes

Apache Kafka can be used in Kubernetes clusters as a reliable event backbone by distributing event streaming platforms. When orchestrated and containerized by Kubernetes:

- Broker instances run as managed pods.
- Persistent volumes ensure message durability.
- Replication mechanisms provide fault tolerance.
- Horizontal scaling supports high-throughput workloads.

Kubernetes manages lifecycle operations such as scaling, self-healing, and rolling updates, ensuring continuous availability of the messaging infrastructure.

Kubernetes-Native Eventing Frameworks

Knative Eventing is a Kubernetes-native event flow management system that offers declarative event flow APIs. Such structures bring in the elements of:

- **Event Sources** – generate events from systems or services.
- **Brokers** – receive and filter events.
- **Triggers** – route events to subscribed consumers.

Events often follow standardized formats such as Cloud Events, enabling interoperability across services and platforms. Configuration is specified in a declarative manner, which means that routing logic can be changed without modifications to application code.

Benefits of Event-Driven Messaging on Kubernetes

Kubernetes event-driven messaging and streaming allow:

- Asynchronous service communication
- Independent service scalability
- Real-time data processing
- Fault-tolerant message delivery
- Support for reactive and microservices-based architectures

Such functions can be useful in the following use cases: real-time analytics, workflow automation, IoT telemetry processing, and large-scale coordination of distributed systems.

4.2 MICROSERVICES INTEGRATION IN CLOUD-NATIVE ENVIRONMENTS

The process of integration of microservices in cloud-native systems represents a paradigm shift in the way the distributed systems are designed, connected, and operated. In comparison to monolithic systems, where components interact at a single codebase, microservices architectures break applications into deployable (autonomous) services. Such services need to communicate via networks, usually between containers, clusters and cloud regions. This makes integration one of the major architectural issues instead of a post-hoc issue.

Cloud-native infrastructure brings with it dynamic nature of infrastructure like container orchestration, autoscaling, ephemeral loads and distributed networking. Such environments should be provided with integration mechanisms to aid service discovery, secure communication, fault tolerance, observability, and scalability. The level of dynamism and scale needed in this case cannot be achieved using traditional methods of point-to-point integration. Rather, the patterns of integration should be in accordance with containerization, orchestration platforms, and declarative models of infrastructure.

Integration in microservice-based systems is done using synchronous and asynchronous communication (e.g. event streams and message brokers). The approaches have varying requirements in their operation. Synchronous calls provide real time communication, whereas asynchronous communication enhances decoupling, resilience and system elasticity. Cloud native integration strategies should strike a balance between the two models and be reliable and performance.

The latest cloud-native systems offer in-built features to make integration of microservices easy. They are service meshes of secure service-to-service communication, API gateways of external access management, event streaming platforms of asynchronous workflow and configuration management systems of dynamic service behavior. These elements combined create an integration fabric used to make distributed systems in cloud-native environments scalable, resilient, and observable.

4.2.1 Synchronous and Asynchronous Communication Patterns

1. **Synchronous Communication**

   In synchronous communication, the caller waits for a response. It is a well-known and popular strategy. It works well in most cases because of its conceptual simplicity, which makes implementation simple.

The HTTP protocol is strongly related to synchronous communication. Nonetheless, there are also other protocols that make sense for implementing synchronous communication. RPC calls are an excellent illustration of an alternative. Other services can call the synchronous interfaces that each component exposes.

The business flow request is intercepted by an interceptor close to the entry point. The request is subsequently forwarded to downstream services. The calls that follow are all synchronous. Until processing is finished, these calls may be made in parallel or sequentially. The way calls are handled within the system can differ. Every call can be specifically orchestrated by an orchestrator. Alternatively, calls may naturally spread among components.

Trade-offs

There are some trade-offs in a distributed configuration, even though synchronous calls are easier to understand, debug, and implement.

- **Balanced capacity:** Deliberate capacity balancing across services is necessary. Requests from downstream services may be overwhelmed by a brief spike at one component. As opposed to asynchronous systems, synchronous communication lacks mediation through queues and can result in cascading failure. Resilience mechanisms such as circuit breakers or bulkhead architecture can help mitigate traffic bursts.
- **Risk of cascading failures:** When downstream services fail or respond slowly, the upstream resources may end up being exhausted at a very fast rate, which spreads around the system in a domino effect. Appropriate timeouts, repeat error management, and SLA implementation are required to lessen impact.
- **Coupling:** Time may be more tightly tied in a synchronous system. Contracts for services directly tie other services, forcing early versioning or propagating contract changes to consumers, increasing system complexity.

Emerging architectural paradigms like service mesh (Istio, Linkerd, Envoy) can address some of these issues by improving fault tolerance and decoupling while maintaining synchronous behavior.

2. **Asynchronous Communication**

Distributed architectures are ideal for asynchronous communication. It decouples the execution of two or more services by eliminating the need to wait for a response. Asynchronous communication can be implemented in a number of ways. Examples include direct RPC (e.g., grpc) or mediating message bus calls to a remote service. Message buses are used as a channel in both event choreography and organized message passing.

Consistent communication and message delivery semantics are two benefits of a central message bus. Compared to direct asynchronous communication between services, this can be a considerable advantage. A message bus or similar media is frequently used to enable consistent cross-service communication.

Trade-offs

Asynchronous service flows can present certain trade-offs and be more difficult to follow throughout the system.

- **Higher system complexity:** Asynchronous systems are significantly more complex. Both orchestrators and components must embrace asynchronous execution.
- **Reads require mediation:** Write-heavy systems are ideally suited for asynchronous architecture systems, but synchronous reads and queries require mediation. Approaches include a synchronous wrapper, CQRS, or dual support for synchronous reads and asynchronous writes. Each introduces additional complexity.
- **Message bus dependency:** The message bus serves as both the system's foundation and a possible source of failure. It must support horizontal scaling.
- **Eventual consistency:** An asynchronous system can be eventually consistent, meaning query results may not reflect the latest writes. This must be considered in system design and user experience.

4.2.2 Service Discovery and Dynamic Configuration Management

The environment of a backend is ever-evolving in a microservices-based application. Cases of service are generated, clustered, updated or canceled dynamically. Due to this volatility, customers are unable to count on fixed IP addresses or manually established points. A service discovery mechanism is a mechanism that allows services to automatically discover and bind to available service instances without any hard coded network knowledge.

Service discovery is an automatic process of finding services in a network. In conventional networking setups, the service discovery protocols were useful in enabling the clients to find compatible devices and resources on demand. This concept has changed in cloud-native systems where distributed workloads based on containers are viewed as dynamically-registered, dynamically-discovered and dynamically-accessible services. Services are based on automated registries and runtime resolutions rather than on the static configuration files.

Service Discovery in Cloud-Native Platforms

The orchestration platform usually takes care of service discovery in the modern cloud-native environments. As an example, Kubernetes offers an implementation of service discovery by giving every Service a stable DNS name and virtual IP address. Scaling and failure modes of pods automatically cause routing updates by Kubernetes so that traffic is sent to healthy instances without client-side reconfiguration.

Service discovery can follow two primary forms:

- Client-side discovery, in which the client does load balancing and requests a service registry to find available service instances.
- Server-side discovery, where an intermediary such as Requests are routed to the relevant service instances by a load balancer or API gateway that queries the registry.

These mechanisms allow distributed services to remain loosely coupled while adapting to runtime changes in infrastructure.

Dynamic Configuration Management

Dynamic configuration management is used to supplement service discovery by moving configuration out of application code. The configuration data like database endpoints, feature flags, credentials, and environment-specific settings, are not supposed to be inbuilt in services in cloud-native systems. Rather, it is centrally stored and administered and injected into services when they run.

Dynamic configuration Platforms like Kubernetes use mechanisms like ConfigMaps and Secrets to provide applications with the ability to change the values of their configuration without rebuilding or redeploying containers. Centralized configuration services also provide runtime updates and therefore, services can be able to adjust to policy changes, scaling events, or environment dissimilarities without requiring downtime.

Benefits in Cloud-Native Microservices

Together, service discovery and dynamic configuration management:

- Eliminate hard-coded service locations
- Enable runtime adaptability
- Support autoscaling and self-healing systems
- Reduce operational complexity
- Improve reliability and resilience

These mechanisms form a critical foundation for scalable and flexible microservices integration in cloud-native environments.

4.2.3 Resilience, Fault Tolerance, and Reliability Mechanisms

1. **Resilience**

   The ability of a distributed system to bounce back and carry on after experiencing malfunctions, outages, or security breaches is known as resilience. High availability does not equate to high resilience; rather, the infrastructure and services are designed to withstand disruptions. In order to reduce the magnitude and duration of disruptive events, resilience is incorporated into business continuity, incident response, and recovery strategies. It is not a stand-alone statistic.

Resiliency can be measured by one of the indicators, namely, the time to repair, which is termed "mean time to repair" (MTTR) and measures the duration of service recovery following failure. Reduced MTTR is a sign of higher resiliency.

The cloud-native systems can be resilient zed with the help of redundancy, failover, autoscaling, and incorporation of software-defined intelligence that is able to automatically detect and heal within a few minutes.

2. **Fault Tolerance**

One of the concepts in the development of resilient microservices is fault tolerance. It makes sure that a system is capable of remaining operational despite failure of some of its components. This is essential in the microservices architectures since applications are based on a combination of interconnected services. Failure of one of the services should not stop the whole application.

There are common strategies and patterns that are applied to reach fault tolerance:

- **Circuit Breaker:** Failed one service: especially when a failure causes other service failures, this prevents the failure of a single service cascading out to other services by preventing request execution once a failure threshold has been met and then recovery time is possible.
- **Retries:** The failed requests are automatically retried with minimal delay, which is helpful when the error is short-term like a temporary network outage. Retries should be regulated to prevent congestion of services.
- **Timeouts**: Makes sure that the system does not wait forever until a response is received. In case a service fails to respond in a given time frame, the request is cancelled.

- **Fallbacks:** Fallback gives different responses in case a service is failing, e.g. fallback data or default value.
- **Rate Limiters:** A rate limiter is used to limit the number of requests that a service can accept in a defined time.

By applying such patterns, it is possible to ensure the availability and reliability of microservices even when failures occur.

3. **Reliability**

Reliability is defined as how likely a given system or service that is being distributed will perform within the specified parameters. A system can be operational over some time but be unable to operate properly, in which case it is less reliable. Reliability refers to infrastructure stability, performance of the service, and predictability when the infrastructure is loaded.

A widely accepted measure that attempts to measure reliability is mean time between failures (MTBF) which is the time interval associated with normal operation inherent failures that are predicted. The bigger the MTBF, the better the reliability.

To enhance reliability, there should be extensive testing to include real-time production situations and edge cases, adequate sizing and configuration of a system, constant monitoring, routine maintenance, and periodic software updates. These are the practices that can be used to make sure that the systems of microservices are stable and reliable in the cloud-native setups.

4.2.4 Observability, Security, and Governance in Distributed Integration

1. **Cloud-Native Observability**

The ability to understand incredibly complex cloud apps and systems—often microservices-based and typically serverless—based on their outcomes and telemetry facts is known as cloud-native observability.

Because it considers the problems of cloud systems, cloud-native observability is an alternative to classical observability. In these systems, containers, virtual computers, and other resources can be created and stopped at any time, generating enormous volumes of data that are sometimes volatile.

In order to support DevOps operations and routine planned upgrades, cloud-native observability solutions can help organisations track key data points in this dynamic environment. Observability platforms collect data across all hybrid clouds, including microservices, in-premises servers, container orchestration platforms like Kubernetes, and services from many providers.

These platforms provide useful information about metrics such as latency and network traffic, as well as how those metrics relate to one another across platforms. Anomaly identification, visualization, and root cause analysis are frequently automated processes. For instance, a cloud-based observability system might collect virtual machine latency measurements, Kubernetes-managed container logs, and network events like application installations, correlate them, and provide the results back to identify the reasons for downtime.

A variety of contemporary observability solutions rely on artificial intelligence and machine learning to help with automation and analysis. The most popular open-source tools are Open Telemetry, Jaeger, and Prometheus that offer flexibility and extensibility in the cloud-native context.

2. **Integration Security**

Integration security is a collection of actions and procedures covering data security when transmitting and processing across various platforms, companies, or departments. It provides safety of data shared between systems that are linked to each other through its lifecycle.

Integration security is implemented at various levels. Encryption of data in transit takes place at the transport layer where protocols like the HTTPS with TLS 1.2 or 1.3 are used. Authentication has been implemented at the application layer, by using OAuth 2.0, JWT tokens and API keys to make sure that only authorized systems and users are allowed to initiate or receive data exchanges.

In the integration pipeline, there are data validation checks to ensure the incoming and outgoing payloads are of the expected format and schema. "Role-based access controls" (RBAC) limit the number of users controlling integrations, modifying synchronization rules, or access to synchronized data. The API calls, data transfers and changes of configuration are monitored to identify anomalies on-the-fly.

These processes can be said to promote three objectives:

- **Data Confidentiality:** Data confidentiality is assured by ensuring that sensitive data is only made available to the appropriate parties by using encryption and through controlled data sharing.
- **Data Integrity**: Data integrity is the ensuring that data has not been altered in any way using hash functions and checksum.
- **Data Availability:** In order to reduce hardware failures, outages, or a cyberattack, data should be easily accessible by means of redundancy, backup, and a retry mechanism.

3. **Governance in Microservices Integration**

There are special requirements when it comes to the implementation of solid data governance in microservices architectures. With the shrinking of monolithic applications to distributed services within organizations, centralized data management methods cannot be used any longer. Each microservice can have its own data storage which can cause possible incompatibility, compliance risks, and security issues.

With microservices architectures, the data has been spread among various autonomous services, possibly with a variety of storage facilities and data models. Unless they are well governed, microservices will turn into data silos, culminating in redundancy, inconsistency, and the inability to have an overall organizational view of data.

Microservices are distributed and this makes tracing data lineage hard because it is difficult to know the flow and transformation of data through services. When data is distributed across a variety of systems, it becomes harder to comply with regulations including GDPR or industry-specific requirements.

A successful data governance offers a structure to resolve these issues and retain the scalability and agility advantages of microservices architectures.It ensures consistent policy enforcement, secure data handling, and operational control across distributed integration environments.

4.3 DATA INTEGRATION, STREAMING, AND SYNCHRONIZATION

The modern cloud-native systems are used to generate and process large amounts of data utilized in distributed services, platforms, and environments. With the implementation of microservices, multi-cloud systems, and event-driven architecture, the importance of seamless data integration is becoming more acute as organizations decide to use them. Data is no longer held in one monolithic database but is distributed throughout the various services, clusters and even geographical locations. To achieve consistency, availability and interoperability between these distributed data sources, there should be effective integration mechanisms.

Cloud-native data integration requires the gathering, conversion, and provision of data between non-homogeneous systems in real time or close to real time. Old batch-based "extract-transform-load" (ETL) pipelines cannot meet the requirements of systems that need continuous updates, low latency and reactive behaviour. Rather, data flows based on streaming architecture, and event-driven operations allow the services to broadcast changes in real-time to support analytics, automation, and responsiveness of operations.

The streaming platforms are the key elements of the contemporary distributed systems functioning as the continuous event backbones. Through these platforms, services can publish and subscribe to event streams which decouples producers and consumers but at the same time, scalable and fault-tolerant data exchange is possible. Streaming is used together with data synchronization mechanisms, which provides state consistency across distributed services, databases, and so on. Absence of proper synchronization mechanisms can introduce inconsistency and staleness of data and conflict of data that will destroy system reliability.

The real-time analytics, cross-service coordination, system resilience, and business continuity are built on a combination of data integration, streaming, and synchronization, which are the elements of cloud-native ecosystems. They enable the organizations to achieve the integrity of data besides offering elasticity, scaling and the processing of data at scale.

4.3.1 Real-Time Data Integration and ETL in Cloud-Native Systems

As the need to be nimbler and more responsive, it has made real-time data integration a differentiator in the contemporary data pipelines. Real-time integration contrasts with batch processing where the operating frequency is specified the data is always in motion and it is processed as new data is made available.

One method used to enable the transfer of data between systems in real-time is the ability to capture, transform, and push data between systems on its creation or modification. These processes are based on streaming technologies and event-driven architecture, so that the insights would be up-to-date, and thus, the decision-making process could operate quickly and with efficiency.

Benefits of Real-Time Data Integration

- **Real-time Intelligence:** Organizations will be able to track important metrics, identify anomalies, and react to events, in real-time.
- **Improved Customer Experience**: Real-time data allows timely, relevant interactions, including an update on the order or dynamic pricing.
- **Operation Agility**: Teams can adapt fast to evolving market conditions or internal operations, and minimize downtime and enhance efficiency.
- **Minimized Data Silos:** Data flow within the organization ensures information is readily available through the servers in the different departments, giving the customers the latest information.

Real-time integration is now more easily done with the help of modern tools and frameworks like Apache Kafka and other cloud-native platforms, offering scalable infrastructure and high-velocity to support data streams.

ETL (Extract, Transform, Load)

ETL (Extract, Transform, Load) is a traditional data integration approach, which is especially useful in structured data and highly data quality and compliance-conscious environments.

- **Extract:** Data is collected from various sources such as databases, APIs, and files.
- **Transform:** Data is cleaned, enriched, and converted into the required format, often on a discrete dispensation waiter.
- **Load:** A data warehouse or analytics platform receives the altered data.

In structured settings where transformation rules and data governance are crucial, such financial reporting or healthcare analytics, ETL is frequently utilised.

Cloud-Native ETL

Cloud-native ETL Cloud-native ETL is ETL tools and processes designed specifically to exploit cloud computing and not on-premises infrastructure.

Cloud computing has a number of benefits.

- **Scalable:** Additional storage or compute resources can be provisioned easily when needed.
- **Mobile-friendly:** Cloud services are accessible from various devices and locations.
- **Fully managed:** Public cloud providers abstract infrastructure management, maintenance, and support responsibilities from users.

Although the core ETL process remains conceptually similar, cloud-native ETL workloads run on remote cloud infrastructure instead of local hardware. This enables improved scalability, operational flexibility, and integration with other cloud services.

4.3.2 Event Streaming Platforms and Message Brokers

The process of gathering real-time data from databases, apps, and Internet of Things devices and sending it to different locations for processing and storage right away or for real-time analysis and analytics reporting is known as event streaming.

By processing data as an event or change occurs, event streaming—a crucial component of "event stream processing" (ESP)—allows IT infrastructures to manage massive, continuous streams of events.

Batch processing, which works with big, static datasets (also known as "data at rest"), is frequently enhanced by event streaming. However, event streaming manages individual data points as they appear rather than processing data in batches. This method enables the architecture's software to analyze and react in real time to data streams, or "data in motion."

From creating real-time machine learning models that identify questionable user behaviour to providing alerts when stock or product prices fluctuate, high-performance event streaming systems may enable a variety of straightforward and intricate activities. By linking events to their corresponding timestamps, event streaming can enhance data analytics even in batch processing. Additionally, it assists in recognizing past patterns, offering insightful information over time.

The distributed architecture that underpins modern computing allows disparate software components—often located in disparate environments—to communicate with one another. In order to enable serverless, microservices, and other cloud-native application architectures, messaging and event streaming are necessary.

From creating real-time machine learning models that identify questionable user behaviour to providing alerts when stock or product prices fluctuate, high-performance event streaming systems may enable a variety of straightforward and intricate activities. By linking events to their corresponding timestamps, event streaming can enhance data analytics even in batch processing. Additionally, it assists in recognizing past patterns, offering insightful information over time.

The distributed architecture that underpins modern computing allows disparate software components—often located in disparate environments—to communicate with one another. In order to enable serverless, microservices, and other cloud-native application architectures, messaging and event streaming are necessary.

- Communication between application components is one of the programming issues brought forth by microservices and other distributed systems. The purpose of message brokers is to offer a standard communication method that adapts to the demands of various applications. Message brokers often include services like translation, routing, persistence, and delivery in addition to messaging, which simplifies communications and lessens the workload for software developers who must manage these features in application code.
- With dependable asynchronous messaging for transmitting events, commands, data, and responses between creating and consuming applications or services, an enterprise-grade message broker aids in ensuring quick, dependable communication across servers, apps, and devices in multi-cloud scenarios. A distributed message broker offers excellent performance, automated management, security, and ease of communication amongst microservices.
- Distributed microservices apps use messages to exchange data with one another. Across many languages and platforms, message brokers can assist in integrating different applications and services. Producers and consumers can send and receive messages independently and at various times without being blocked thanks to asynchronous messaging.

4.3.3 Data Consistency, Replication, and Synchronization Strategies

1. **Data Consistency in Microservices**

   In a microservices architecture, ensuring data consistency across distributed services is a critical challenge. Unlike monolithic systems, where a single database enforces consistency, microservices often maintain separate databases, leading to eventual consistency scenarios.

   1. **Saga Pattern:** The Saga pattern orchestrates a series of local transactions across microservices, ensuring consistency without relying on distributed transactions. The services do their work and produce an event to establish the next one. In case of a step failure, the compensating actions revert previous actions.
   2. **Event Sourcing:** Event Sourcing maintains a system's status as an event sequence as opposed to data snapshots. Every event signifies a change in state and the present state is obtained through being replayed. This guarantees uniformity in services as there is one source of truth.
   3. **CQRS (Command Query Responsibility Segregation):** Read and write operations are separated into distinct models by CQRS to enable the optimization of data management of each one. In microservices, this is often combined with Event Sourcing to achieve consistency with the read and write databases.
   4. **Compensating Transactions:** Transaction Compensation (or Compensating actions) offer a way to reverse the changes in case a distributed transaction fails. They are also based on application-level logic in order to undo operations unlike ACID transactions and are frequently combined with the Saga pattern.

2. **Data Replication in Microservices**

   There is no bug of data replication in the world of microservices, but it is a feature. As systems become increasingly complex and large, the necessity to have services to duplicate data becomes not just widespread but is architecturally necessary. However, with this requirement come a number of issues: consistency trade-offs, schema drift, and the risk of stale data always exists. The complexity of replication is essential to designing resilient, performant, and autonomous services that cloud-native architects and CTOs need to take into account when designing cloud-native systems.

3. **Synchronization Strategies**

   The data synchronization provides that the replicated or distributed data will be synchronized across the services and systems over time. To control consistency trade-offs and avert the stale data conditions in distributed environments, synchronization mechanisms are required.

   Event-driven updates, replication, and coordination patterns are often used to provide synchronization in microservices architecture in order to propagate changes between services and tolerate system failure and performance.

4.3.4 Change Data Capture (CDC) and Event-Driven Data Propagation

Conventional data movement involves the use of an "Extract, Transform, Load" (ETL) tool to retrieve a source data and transform it, and insert it into a destination database. This process can be a defined cache window, therefore, restricting the frequency of data transfer.

Conversely, a CDC system transmits changes in data on a real-time basis. This maintains systems in check and offers a sure way of data replication, enabling the cloud migration of zero-downtime of cloud architecture making CDC highly compatible with current cloud architecture.

Managing ongoing source data updates, which might cause discrepancies between the source and target systems, is a major difficulty in this situation. It is challenging to ensure timely updates and data accuracy throughout the whole ETL pipeline because of these issues.

In order to overcome these difficulties, CDC records changes in the source database in real time, enabling the target system to replicate just the modified data. CDC makes it possible for changes to be propagated as events when paired with an event-driven architecture. This can cause the target system to process and synchronise in real-time. By doing this, latency is decreased and the target system is kept current without requiring full data extractions.

In event-driven microservices architecture, CDC has emerged as a crucial tactic for connecting contemporary cloud-native applications with conventional databases.

While CDC records database-level data modifications (such as inserts, updates, and deletes), it requires a messaging mechanism to spread those changes to pertinent microservices. Treating the modifications as events in an event-driven architecture and sending them asynchronously is the most effective approach to achieve this.

4.4 MULTI-CLOUD AND HYBRID INTEGRATION STRATEGIES

In the contemporary business, the operation is hardly a one-cloud or infrastructure environment. Instead of that, they are shifting to multi-cloud and hybrid architecture in order to establish the balance in performance, cost, regulatory compliance, geographic dispersion, and vendor flexibility. The distribution of the workloads by organizations between the public clouds, the private clouds and the on-premise data centers itself renders the process of integration very complex. Integration strategies will be effectively defined in these heterogeneous environments to facilitate smooth communication, consistency of data and operational visibility in these environments.

Multi-cloud strategy entails the utilization of multiple cloud companies, including the deployment of applications in various public cloud companies. The strategy saves the vendor lock-in, enhances resilience, and enables organizations to take advantage of the best-of-breed services of each vendor. Nonetheless, it presents networking, identity management and observability, security policy issues, and portability of data.

A hybrid solution to cloud deployment merges in-premise systems with a public cloud system. There are numerous businesses that have old systems, regulatory binds, or workloads that are latency aware that simply cannot be fully moved to the cloud. These systems are hybrid-integrated to be interoperable with cloud-native applications, APIs, along with data pipelines. This is possible by enabling secure connectivity, workload orchestration, and a uniform environment governance.

The strategies that are effective in multi-cloud and hybrid integration are based on standardized APIs, containerization, service mesh, API gateways, central identity, and cloud-agnostic deployment models. With these mechanisms, portability, scalability and uniformity of operations can be achieved with minimal fragmentation across the distributed infrastructure environments.

4.4.1 Cloud-Agnostic Architecture and Portability Strategies

An strategy to developing, implementing, and managing software that allows the same workload to run on several public cloud providers with very slight, scripted modifications is known as cloud-agnostic architecture.

Strict abstraction layers, vendor-neutral tooling, and open standards are used to achieve portability. This cloud-agnostic method maintains optionality while giving parity precedence over extensive integration.

Cloud-agnostic apps can "plug into" any cloud provider (AWS, Azure, GCP) with little change, just as a universal power adapter can be used in any country's electrical outlets.

The ability to transfer workloads, data, apps, and services between cloud computing platforms with no interruption, incompatibility, or setup modifications is known as portability. IT teams may move cloud workloads between different public, private, multicloud, and hybrid cloud environments, as well as between different cloud providers, thanks to cloud portability. Resources such as virtual machines, containers, and data can be readily redeployed or replicated across many platforms and cloud providers thanks to cloud portability. This enables the IT teams to optimize performance for each workload, minimize costs, and avoid vendor lock-in.

In cloud computing, there are various types of portability.

- **Application portability** is the capacity to quickly transfer apps between various cloud environments or platforms without causing incompatibilities or necessitating major modifications to the code, design, or configuration of the application.

- **Data portability** is the capacity to move data while preserving integrity, consistency, and usability between various cloud environments or service providers.
- **Workload portability** is the capacity to move workloads, such as virtual machines, containers, or service functionalities, between cloud environments or providers without affecting performance or functionality.
- **Platform portability** is the capacity to transfer whole cloud platforms or specific parts, such as middleware, runtime environments, and operating systems, between clouds or cloud providers.

Best ways to achieve portability

To achieve portability, IT teams and organisations can follow a number of best practices.

- **Adopt cloud native architectures**: By separating apps from particular underlying technology, cloud native designs like microservices and containerization make them more adaptable to many cloud environments. Because of their open standards and modular design, cloud native apps are by nature more portable.
- **Leverage open standards and APIs**: Interoperability between systems and portability among cloud providers are made easier by the use of open source technologies, open standards for data formats, and well-documented application programming interfaces (APIs).
- **Utilize containerization**: Applications can move across environments thanks to container technologies like Kubernetes.
- **Implement automation and orchestration**: IT teams may automate and manage the use of containerized apps with the use of orchestration solutions like Rancher, HashiCorp, and OpenShift.
- **Deploy open source, cloud-agnostic tools and services**: Platforms, services, and tools that are cloud-agnostic are made

to function flawlessly across a variety of cloud environments, removing reliance on particular cloud providers and simplifying migration.

- **Invest in cloud skills and expertise**: IT teams will be competent in managing and transferring workloads across many cloud environments if they concentrate on building internal skills and knowledge in cloud technology.

4.4.2 Cross-Cloud Networking, Security, and Identity Federation

The basic elements Identity federation, security, and cross-cloud networking are features of multi-cloud and hybrid integration designs. With more and more work being divided between different providers of on-premises systems and public and private clouds, performance, compliance, and resilience across all environments become necessary, and seamless and secure connectivity is key.

1. **Cross-Cloud Networking**

   Multi-cloud and hybrid cloud setup needs to have safe and effective networking amidst dissimilar systems. Secure cross-cloud networking helps to provide a method of communication between applications and services between various cloud platform without data integrity/performance compromise. This can include encrypted tunnels, virtual private networks (VPNs), dedicated connection (like AWS Direct Connection or Azure Express Route), and overlay networking (that expand secure network segments across clouds).

   The design of the cross-cloud network should consider the disparities between the cloud providers and the on-prem infrastructure, and safe data flows across the general internet or internal backbone connections. A strong architecture can shield the access by unauthorized personnel as well as facilitate free traffic movement across all the settings.

2. **Security Across Multi-Cloud and Hybrid Environments**

   Hybrid and multi-cloud security is concerned with the security of data, identities, workloads, and network traffic when traversing environments. Due to the workloads cutting across different fields perimeter-based security can no longer be applied. Rather, the security strategies need to offer a unified visibility, uniformity in policy implementation, and concerted threat identification of all infrastructures linked together.

The fundamental components of cross-cloud security are the data confidentiality and integrity, safe network fragmentation, uniform configuration and access policies, and real-time monitoring. Security teams should deal with the issues of greater attack surfaces, configuration drift, and policy gaps that occur when various clouds adopt various tools and control planes.

3. **Identity Federation and Unified Access**

Identity federation enables users to and services to gain access to resources in many cloud environments with the use of one trusted identity. In a multi-cloud or hybrid system, some "Identity and Access Management" (IAM) systems need to be extended to operate with federated identity protocols that enable the safe operation of authentication and authorization across heterogeneous systems: SAML, OAuth 2.0 and OpenID connect.

Federated identity offers single-sign-on (SSO) across cloud providers and easy access control of distributed applications, vendors, partners, and subsidiaries. This model lessens the proliferation of credentials, enhances usability, and tightens security by concentrating trust affiliations and permits domain-decentralized authentication.

Coherent identity approaches together with reliable networking and coherent security policies will guarantee that cloud-native applications that are executed within a variety of domains can safely inter-operate and have a seamless operation without interfering with user access controls and regulations.

4.4.3 Data Integration and Consistency Across Hybrid Environments

When at least one data source or platform is cloud-based, cloud data integration refers to the procedures and tools used to integrate and harmonise data across platforms.

As part of a larger business data management strategy, cloud data integration aims to enhance cloud data access and delivery throughout the company while maintaining data security, governance, and performance. These fundamental skills are especially crucial as businesses seek to apply AI, improve customer satisfaction, and advance real-time analytics at a time when data volume, speed, and scale are all increasing at an exponential rate.

The umbrella of the cloud data integration encompasses two subtypes, which are hybrid cloud data integration and multicloud data integration.

- **Hybrid cloud data integration:** This is an integration that incorporates data in the public cloud, a private cloud and on-premises data.
- **Multicloud data integration:** Multicloud data integration combines data stored in cloud services by two or more cloud providers.

Most businesses nowadays are running in hybrid multicloud environments that overlap both services of the public and the private cloud. Cloud data integration forms the basis of data access, reliance and utility in any location it is stored in this model.

The hybrid cloud data integration is the process of bringing together data that can be found in different locations on-premise databases, cloud-based services, and SaaS applications together into a unified, accessible, and secure system. It is also essential to business that is focused on taking advantage of the full range of analytics, business intelligence, and decision-making abilities of their hybrid environments.

Integration Strategies for Hybrid Environments

- **Selection of the appropriate Integration Platform:** Select a Hybrid Integration Platform, which can be used to implement a broad set of integration patterns, such as real-time, batch, and event-driven integrations. This scalability is essential towards meeting the varying data requirements of a hybrid cloud setup.

- **Focusing on Data Security and Compliance:** Make sure that the integration solutions comply with the industry standards and regulations. This involves the use of strong encryption, identity controls, and access controls to ensure the sensitive information safety.
- **Using APIs to achieve Smooth Interconnectedness:** APIs are very vital in hybrid integrations and they allow interconnectedness of various services and platforms in a secure and efficient way. An API-first approach will help with a smoother integration and scalability.
- **Automating Data Integration Processes:** Automation tools are capable of playing a major role in alleviating manual labor in data integration process of data, and in making sure that data is available in the system at the right time and with the right accuracy. Not only does this increase efficiency but it also decreases chances of errors.

Key Considerations for Hybrid Cloud Data Integration

- **Data Management and Quality**: Good data management practices are essential in making sure that the integrated data is correct, constant and dependable. This includes the use of data quality control, metadata control and data governance rules.
- **Cloud Computing and Scalability**: The selected integration solutions must be able to scale to meet increasing data volumes and changing workloads without affecting the performance or the security.
- **Overcoming Integration problems:** Hybrid cloud environments can be characterized by each peculiar integration problem, including data latency, compatibility, and sophisticated security needs. These issues need to be expected and overcome.
- **Data Migration Strategies**: In the case of businesses which are moving to the hybrid cloud model, the strategic data migration plan is crucial. This includes selecting the appropriate migration methods, such as lift-and-shift, refactoring, or replatforming, based on the specific needs and goals of the organization.

4.4.4 Operational Governance, Observability, and Cost Management

Operation governance is used to make sure that cloud resources are deployed in a controlled, secure and compliant way on a variety of platforms in a multi-cloud and hybrid environment. Governance entails policy, procedure, and control on how infrastructure, applications and data is provisioned, accessed, monitored and maximized. It gives responsibility to the utilization of resources but also makes sure that the standards are met in terms of regulations, security, and organization.

Heightened cloud governance systems characterize proprietorship devices, role-based duties, and automatized policy violation systems. The controls assist in the prevention of configuration drifts, the implementation of security foundations, and the consistency of environments. Governance in Multi-cloud and hybrid environments must be distributed among and inside on-premises, private, and public clouds infrastructure to guarantee coherent system operation.

- **Observability Across Hybrid and Multi-Cloud Environments**

  Observability allows organizations to learn about the behavior of systems using telemetry data which includes logs, metrics and traces. Unified observability is essential in distributed environments spanning several on-premises systems and cloud providers to guarantee security, dependability, and performance.

  The hybrid and multi-cloud observability solutions combine the telemetry data of various environments into centralized monitors. This consolidated visibility enables the teams to identify anomalies, diagnosis, and bottlenecks in the performance and also do root cause analysis in real time. Operational blind spots may arise between fragmented cloud environments without the unified observability.

- **Cost Management and FinOps**

  The multi-cloud and hybrid approaches necessitate cost management due to the complex billing and variable consumption patterns in distributed deployments. The idea of cloud cost optimization is dedicated to knowing spending habits, killing unutilized resources, downsizing the infrastructure, and synchronizing the cloud investment with the business goals.

A newer field of operational management that contributes to cost management is FinOps, which facilitates the use of collaboration across an engineering, a financial, and a business team. The FinOps practices include focusing on cost visibility and accountability in real-time and making decisions based on data in order to ensure the maximization of the value of cloud investments without interfering with performance and scalability.

Combined, the operational governance, observability, and cost management offer the control layer on the multi-cloud and hybrid integration strategies. They guarantee the distributed cloud-native systems to be secure, efficient, and transparent and strike a balance between compliance, performance, and financial sustainability.

4.5 SECURITY, IDENTITY, AND ZERO-TRUST INTEGRATION

Enterprise systems are becoming less perimeter-based in their architecture, as more distributed, cloud-native, and API-driven systems are developed, which can no longer be viewed as security. Conventional models supposed a secure internal network and insecure external environment. Nevertheless, contemporary integration architectures cut across the public clouds, private clouds, partner ecosystems, mobile clients, IoT devices as well as the edge infrastructure. The concept of identity, authentication, and unremitting verification turns out to be the pillars of secure integration in this landscape.

The current definition of integration security should safeguard data during transit, implement the least-privileged access, authenticate the machine-to-machine interactions, and trace the interactions between distributed services. The APIs, service meshes, event streams, and cross-cloud networks establish numerous trust boundaries that need to be developed dynamically. Network firewalls and static access controls will not be effective in microservices with high dynamics.

Zero-trust architecture deals with the challenges that all users, services and devices must not be trusted without question even when they are within the network environment. All requests should be verified, checked, and constantly verified. Identity has become the new security boundary, and enforcement of policy should be achieved consistently across APIs, containers, workloads and integration pipelines.

Enterprise integration architecture is based on a layer of security, identity control and zero-trust principles. They guarantee that distributed systems can withstand the changing cyber threats as well as enabling scalability, interoperability, and compliance under hybrid and multi-cloud conditions.

4.5.1 Identity and Access Management (IAM) in Cloud-Native and Distributed Systems

Only authorized identities are granted access to the appropriate resources thanks to "identity and access management" (IAM). IAM serves as the new perimeter in cloud-native security, shielding sensitive resources from misuse and unauthorised access as cloud platforms combine various administrative tasks of data centers and services into unified web consoles and "application programming interfaces" (APIs) that are accessible over the Internet.

Identity and Access Management in Domain 5 is covered in the Cloud Security Alliance's Security Guidance v5.0. "Cloud service providers" (CSPs) and "cloud service customers" (CSCs) are responsible for administering IAM within reasonable risk tolerances in both public and private clouds. Although basic IAM concepts will be reviewed, the emphasis will be on the features and difficulties of IAM in the cloud and how to handle them effectively. Neither the CSP nor the CSC can handle IAM on their own. Both parties must have a relationship based on trust, clearly define roles, and have the technical know-how to manage it.

Cloud-Native Identity & Access Management

Cloud-native IAM is the collection of procedures, guidelines, and tools intended to control and safeguard access, rights, and identities within Cloud-native environments. In contrast to IAM solutions that were traditionally based on products that aim at on-premises systems, Cloud-native IAM solutions are designed to meet the specific demands of dynamic, distributed cloud environments.

The Importance of Cloud-native IAM

1. **Security and Compliance:** Cloud-native IAM is critical to securing data, regulatory compliance, and cloud governance. Organizations can prevent security threats and ensure that regulatory requirements are met by implementing the granular access controls, authentication schemes, and audit trails.

2. **Scalability and Flexibility:** Cloud-native IAM solutions are scalable and flexible to manage the growing user demands, application patterns and access regulations that organizations need as their operations grow and scale. This can be scaled to provide a smooth access control across a wide range of cloud services and availability.

3. **Improved User Experience**: Frictionless access to resources, applications, and services with high security standards is an improved user experience that can be offered by an effective Cloud-native IAM. This tradeoff of security and user experience creates productivity and user disposition.

Challenges in Cloud-native IAM Implementation

1. **Complexity**: Cloud-native environments are distributed and dynamic, and this brings complexity to IAM implementation. Controlling identities, permissions, and access on many cloud platforms, services, and microservices architectures may be difficult.

2. **Integration:** To deploy Cloud-native IAM solutions in conjunction with on-premises system, legacy applications, and third-party services, there must be a smooth interoperability and compatibility. Having a holistic IAM coverage requires clear integration.

3. **Security Risks**: Cloud-native IAM provides new security threats that include misconfigurations, insider threats, and unauthorized access because of the spread of cloud services and decentralized access controls. It is required to implement proactive threat detection and mitigation strategies.

Best Practices for Effective Cloud-native IAM

1. **Zero-Trust Security Model:** Use a Zero-Trust Security model that identifies all access requests irrespective of the location of the user or network segment. Use granular access controls, least privilege, and persistent authentication in order to reduce security risks.
2. **Identity Federation**: Use Identity Federation protocols, such as OAuth (Open Authorization) and "Security Assertion Mark-up Language" (SAML), to facilitate identity federation over cloud services and apps in a safe and easy manner. This enhances the user experience and promotes Single Sign-On (SSO).
3. **Automated Provisioning and De-provisioning**: Automate the provisioning and de-provisioning of systems to simplify the User Lifecycle Management. Provide access rights according to roles, responsibilities, and organizational changes in time, and revoke access promptly in case of offboarding users.
4. **Multifactor Authentication (MFA):** Activate "Multifactor authentication" (MFA) i.e. biometrics, SMS codes or hardware tokens to introduce an additional protection when doing the authentication. MFA eliminates the threat of unauthorized access and improves Identity Verification.

4.5.2 Zero-Trust Architecture and Policy Enforcement

"Zero Trust Architecture" (ZTA) is a contemporary approach to cybersecurity that is developed on the basis of one main idea: never trust, always verify. Contrary to the traditional security models which presuppose that all that is inside the perimeter is secure, ZTA assumes that all users, devices and applications are not trusted by default, both inside and outside the network.

The network has reduced attack surface, prevented lateral movement and ensured the protection of critical assets in a highly distributed digital environment by continuously authenticating and authorizing all access requests.

- **Core Principles of Zero Trust Architecture**

  One noteworthy design that offers a very unique perspective and method for cybersecurity is zero trust. Its fundamental tenet is that confidence must be gained over time rather than automatically given based on network position at a specific moment. The zero-trust security model is based on five fundamental principles:

- **Never Trust, Always Verify**

  No entity on any network, be it a user, task, device, external party, or even an on-premises entity, is ever assumed to be trustworthy. As will be covered in more detail below, each access request needs to be validated using a variety of criteria.

- **Least-Privileged Access**

  Only the precise resource that an authorized user requires (right now) to finish a particular job should be made available to them. To put it another way, people who have valid access needs ought to be linked directly to applications rather than the network itself, which would allow them to move laterally and access other network-connected resources.

- **Contextual and Risk-Based Access Governance**

  By examining the context of each access request, zero trust continuously assesses risk. This is accomplished by using AI/ML to examine contextual factors such as user behaviour, device posture/health, geolocation, time of day, and more. Access to IT resources is then controlled by this risk calculation.

Continuous Monitoring and Risk Adaptation

Zero trust uses real-time risk identification through ongoing monitoring of all transactions. Trust isn't static thanks to this dynamic analysis. The zero-trust platform must be able to adapt dynamically and implement different policies based on the access circumstance.

- **No Public IP Addresses**

  Services and data that they have not expressly allowed should not be discovered by unauthorized users and devices. To that effect, zero trust means protecting the internet apps against the eyes of monitors. That is, the removal of public IP addresses and the exchange of inbound connections with inside-out connections to aid in reducing the attack surface.

Following these principles, zero trust allows organizations to reduce the risk, decrease the complexity and enhance the security of their distributed environments.

"Zero-Trust Architectures" (ZTA) policy enforcement is a principle upon which behaviour in the management of digital resource access is based, ground-level. Contrary to the old models of network security that were mainly based on the use of perimeter-based security and non-dynamic rules, Zero-Trust places the emphasis of security on dynamic and continuous assessment of trust. Here, policy enforcement is not a gatekeeping activity but a continuing, context sensitive process that assesses users, devices and data flows in real-time. It entails specifying granular access control policies according to attributes like identity, device posture, location and sensitivity of the requested resource. These policies are implemented with a central "Policy Decision Point" (PDP) and implemented with "Policy Enforcement Points" (PEPs), who are gatekeepers at the different nodes within the network. This structure enables uniformity of security controls in the application irrespective of the location of users or services.

4.5.3 API Security, Service Mesh Security, and Secure Communication

The activity of avoiding or reducing assaults on application programming interfaces (APIs) is known as "API security." APIs serve as the online and mobile applications' backend framework. As a result, safeguarding the private information people send is essential.

An API specifies how various software programs communicate with one another. It regulates the kinds of requests that are made between programs, how they are made, and the types of data formats that are utilised. Websites and "Internet of Things" (IoT) apps both employ APIs.

They frequently collect and process data or let the user enter data that is handled inside the API's host environment.

For instance, Google Maps is run via an API. Google Maps can be integrated into a page that a web designer is creating. When a user accesses Google Maps, they are merely utilising a prewritten API that Google has provided, rather than the code that the web designer-built piece by piece. Both the APIs you directly use and those you indirectly use are covered by API security.

Main takeaways about service mesh security:

- A service mesh uses automatic mTLS encryption and distributed proxies to enable secure and seamless communication across microservices.
- Service meshes enforce zero trust policies and keep security logic apart from application code since they deploy as an infrastructure layer with sidecar proxies.
- Service meshes provide many benefits, but they also have many drawbacks, such as security threats, configuration difficulties, and performance overhead. High access limits, automation, and lightweight proxies can all help with these issues.

A layer of the infrastructure designed to securely enable communication between your microservices is called a service mesh. It uses a distributed network of lightweight proxies, and you may utilise a toolset that helps you with traffic routing, exchange assurance, and traceability, rather than the application code handling network problems.

Your microservices system may quickly go mushy without a service mesh in the mix - every team will need to implement API security independently (consider inconsistent authentication and authorization, sporadic traffic encryption, and a lot of duplicate logic in error handling and routing). Stated differently, a service mesh not only saves time but simplifies logic as it focuses transport security and policy on all microservices.

However, alongside all the benefits, service meshes are very large security burdens in their own right. Control plane is such an appealing place to attackers: To interfere with it is to control the whole service ecosystem. Also, misconfigurations are quite typical and a single incorrect authorization policy may reveal sensitive services or interrupt valid traffic patterns.

Secure Communication Techniques

- **Mutual TLS (mTLS):** The mutually authenticates two services with certificates issued by a reliable Certificate Authority. It has the effect of encrypting traffic, and authenticating both the identity of the client and the server.
- **OpenID Connect (OIDC):** OIDC is a single sign-on (SSO) and authentication based on OAuth2. JWT tokens are issued to authenticating users and these are checked by services to permit access.
- **Authorization and Policy Enforcement:** Authorization is used to find out if an authenticated entity is permitted to access a resource. By decoupling authorization logic with a Policy Decision Point (e.g., OPA), fine-grained services can be given a centralized policy enforcement.
- **Service Mesh-Based Security:** Service meshes are traffic-secured east-west with sidecar proxies and auto-managed mTLS, and they do not require application code modification.

Multiple Choice Questions (MCQs)

1. **What is the primary role of Kubernetes in cloud-native integration platforms?**

   A. Managing hardware resources

   B. Automating deployment, scaling, and management of containerized applications

   C. Designing relational databases

   D. Creating programming languages

2. **Which architectural approach enables applications to be built as small, independent services in cloud-native environments?**

   A. Monolithic Architecture

   B. Client-Server Model

   C. Microservices Architecture

   D. Waterfall Model

3. **In microservices integration, which technology is commonly used for communication between services?**

   A. SOAP only

   B. Message queues or APIs

   C. FTP servers

   D. Manual data transfer

4. **What is the primary purpose of data streaming in distributed systems?**

   A. Storing large datasets offline

   B. Processing real-time data continuously

   C. Compressing files

   D. Managing user authentication

5. **Which tool is widely used for real-time data streaming and event processing?**

   A. Apache Kafka

   B. MySQL

   C. Microsoft Word

   D. Adobe Photoshop

6. **What does hybrid integration refer to in enterprise systems?**
   A. Integration of only on-premise systems
   B. Integration of cloud and on-premise environments
   C. Integration of mobile devices only
   D. Integration of software with hardware

7. **Which strategy helps organizations avoid vendor lock-in by using services from multiple cloud providers?**
   A. Private Cloud Strategy
   B. Multi-Cloud Strategy
   C. Local Deployment Strategy
   D. Standalone Infrastructure Strategy

8. **What is the main principle of Zero-Trust Security in distributed systems?**
   A. Trust all internal network users
   B. Trust users after login only
   C. Never trust, always verify
   D. Disable authentication

9. **Which technology is commonly used to manage identity and access in cloud environments?**
   A. Identity and Access Management (IAM)
   B. File Transfer Protocol (FTP)
   C. Simple Mail Transfer Protocol (SMTP)
   D. Hypertext Transfer Protocol (HTTP)

10. **Why is synchronization important in distributed data integration?**
    - A. To ensure consistent and updated data across systems
    - B. To reduce application development cost
    - C. To eliminate databases
    - D. To stop network communication

Answers

1	2	3	4	5	6	7	8	9	10
B	C	B	B	A	B	B	C	A	A

5

Governance, Compliance, and Future Trends

5.1 COMPLIANCE-DRIVEN AND AUDIT-READY ARCHITECTURES

The intensity of regulatory expectations across industries remains strong, as organizations operate in distributed, cloud-native, and data-driven environments. The regulations like GDPR, HIPAA, SOC 2, ISO 27001, PCI-DSS, and industry-specific requirements do not merely mandate compliance with the policies but they also mandate that the compliance be proven and demonstrable. In this regard, compliance is no longer a fringe governance practice; it is now an architectural issue (Alawami, 2022).

Traditionally, compliance activities were responsive. Organizations which are ready to undergo audits regularly by gathering logs, compiling documentation, and manually verifying controls just before the regulatory reviews. This methodology might have operated in the old in-premise and static systems, but it is not scalable in new architectures where deployment is continuous, infrastructure is transient, and there are microservices and distributed platforms. The physical evidence collection process is prone to errors, costly, and disruptive to operations.

Compliance architecture changes the attitude from reacting to reports to anticipating design. In lieu of retrofitting controls once systems are deployed, compliance requirements are directly implemented in infrastructure provisioning, identity management, logging systems, data handling processes, and deployment pipelines. Factors such as governance, security, and regulatory constraints are considered first-class design inputs rather than external checklists.

Audit-ready architectures build on this idea by ensuring that systems continually generate, store, and verify evidence of compliance in real time. Controls are controlled, logs are non-mutable, access can be traced and policy is codified. Organizations do not plan audits at specific times, but they remain in constant readiness and produce evidence whenever required, without interrupting operations.

Contemporary compliance-focused systems prioritize enforcement over periodic verification. With automation, policy-as-code, infrastructure-as-code, observability tooling, and centralized governance platforms, organisations can guarantee consistency in compliance across development, staging, and production environments. The method minimizes risk exposure, eliminates configuration drift, promotes accountability, and increases transparency.

Enterprises can avoid the need to retrofit compliance into their systems by designing compliance into the architecture instead of adding it as an afterthought, enabling them to produce systems that are defensible, resilient, and scalable to regulatory compliance. Compliance is a facilitator of trust and operational stability rather than a limiting factor on innovation. Audit-ready is not a requirement in highly regulated industries, but it is also a competitive advantage.

5.1.1 Compliance By Design: Embedding Controls into Architecture

The process of creating systems that use their architecture to impose governance is known as compliance by design. After deployment, controls are not added on top. They are integrated into data flow, decision tracking, and service operations.

This starts during the design stage. Not throughout the audit period.

Workflows for provisioning are shaped by it. It outlines the management of access and identity. It guarantees that each system operation generates a record that can be independently verified.

Designing compliance makes important behaviour automatic.

- As users engage with services, logs are generated.
- Roles and context are used to manage permissions.
- In real time, exceptions are reported.

This is not an overlay. It is a property of the structure.

It enables systems to demonstrate their functionality under duress, during audits, and in situations where trust needs to be gained right away.

Architecture Make Systems Audit-Ready

Pulling logs when the auditor shows up is not the goal of audit readiness. It's about knowing that your system can demonstrate its functionality at any time and without additional effort.

The guesswork in governance is eliminated when architecture is built to reveal proof of access, activities, choices, and exceptions. There is a record for each request. Each process corresponds to a policy. Each integration adheres to data controls that are verifiable without manual tracking.

This is what distinguishes structurally accountable systems from reactive compliance.

A system's architecture establishes its ability to:

- Track the ancestry of data across services
- Connect access logs to certain events and roles.
- Real-time flagging of unauthorised activity
- Without human involvement, package activity records for auditing.

Compliance changes from fire drill to feature when these features are included in the build (not added later).

Key Elements of Modern Compliance Strategy

Compliance in the modern era is not a document or dashboard. It is a collection of architectural requirements that enable a system to demonstrate its integrity in any setting and at any time.

Different industries have different conditions. However, the most robust systems have a set of structural capabilities in common:

1. **Constant Access Control:** Context defines permissions. The system uses both user tiers and their current roles and geographic location and their current workload and real-time status to determine access rights.
2. **Integrated Policy Enforcement:** Services include built-in policies that regulate their operations. The system handles these elements through automatic activation, which occurs during workflow execution, infrastructure template use, and API call deployment.
3. **Structured Audit Trails:** System-specific log silos do not exist within the system. The logs exist because they link to particular identities who display specific behaviour and they contain timestamps and they follow standard formats.
4. **Observability at the Correct Level:** Dashboards show two types of noncompliant behavior, which include policy violations and unauthorized access incidents, together with ongoing activities. Risk owners can access operational data through their rights of full visibility.
5. **Data Lifecycle Control**: The organization manages its data lifecycle from creation to deletion through coding programs instead of using spreadsheets, which operate according to business rules and legal requirements and protect consumer rights.

The combination of these elements' changes compliance from a reporting obligation into a fundamental design principle.

Architectural Risks and Compliance Failure Patterns

The most systems pass their audits because they have sufficient controls to meet requirements. The controls fail to function because no one can provide evidence of their operational effectiveness in actual production environments.

The hidden nature of early warning indicators emerges from organizations that separate their architectural work from their compliance duties. The structural risk trends that lead to audit discoveries begin to emerge long before the actual audits take place.

1. **Access That Can't Be Explained:** Risk develops hidden risks due to the practice of distributing tasks through manual methods, which only receive updates after long periods, and which distribute work across different systems without any centralized decision-making process.
2. **Logs Without Lineage:** Logs become non-auditable records that contain activity details because they lack connections to specific users and services and timestamps.
3. **Manual Audit Prep:** Your system is not truly "ready" if teams are still spending a significant portion of time manually combing through log data, creating custom queries, and amassing spreadsheets to validate compliance.

5.1.2 Continuous Compliance and Monitoring for Audit Readiness

Continuous compliance is a process of regularly checking that policies and controls align with relevant regulatory frameworks, standards, and internal governance requirements. Continuous compliance involves regular checks of systems, settings, and operations, rather than a one-time assessment, to ensure weaknesses and noncompliance are identified as they occur.

Continuous controls monitoring can be defined as the application of technology-based solutions to automate the monitoring of compliance, risk management, and security controls. By automatically validating control states, organizations will be able to identify, fix, and prevent control failures on the fly rather than learning about them during periodic audits. This will help to eliminate the need to use manual sampling and make governance more reliable.

Continuous auditing is the automatic and regular review of controls, processes and transactions by audit functions. Technology enhances the timeliness and accuracy of assurance activities by identifying exceptions, anomalies, or control failures as they happen. Audit evidence will be created as a result of regular work processes and not as a compilation, as automated checks are added to operational systems.

Monitoring is a process and technology used to identify compliance and risk issues related to organizational operations and controls. It analyses the system's transactions and activity in real time and finds errors, policy breaches, and new risks. This shifts compliance from a reactive remediation to proactive risk management.

Together, continuous compliance, continuous controls monitoring, continuous auditing, and continuous monitoring make structurally audit-ready systems. Evidence is produced continuously, control drift is detected at the first stage, and compliance validation is incorporated into the working process rather than considered a periodic task.

5.1.3 Governance Evolution and the Future of Regulatory Architecture

The regulatory and governance models are undergoing a major transformation as digital systems become more sophisticated, decentralized, and self-directed. The outdated compliance methods such as manual reviews, fixed policies, and regular audits are being substituted by the technology-based governance frameworks that allow maintaining constant control, automation, and real-time monitoring.

The current regulatory design is moving towards incorporating the latest developments in cloud computing, machine learning, artificial intelligence, and distributed systems to enhance its capacity to govern and manage risks.

1. **The Rise of Regulatory Technology (RegTech)**

   Regulatory Technology (RegTech) is the application of modern technologies to automate and improve the quality of regulatory work. It uses automation, analytics based on big data and cloud computing to enhance monitoring, reporting and compliance validation.

   RegTech solutions help organizations:

   - Automate compliance checks and reporting

- Improve fraud detection and risk identification
- Maintain structured audit trails
- Reduce operational costs associated with manual compliance

RegTech will enable compliance to become reactive rather than proactive governance by integrating regulatory controls into digital systems.

2. **AI Governance and Emerging Regulatory Frameworks**

With the increasing autonomy of artificial intelligence systems and their widespread use, governments and international organizations are developing regulatory frameworks to enforce responsible AI use.

Emerging AI governance frameworks emphasize:

- Transparency and explainability
- Human oversight and accountability
- Data governance and protection
- Risk-based classification of AI systems

This shift can be considered a transition towards a jurisdiction- and risk-sensitive regulatory architecture that organizations will need to incorporate directly into the design of their systems.

3. **Unified Governance, Risk, and Compliance (GRC) Platforms**

The integrated GRC platforms are more or less a trend as modern enterprises are implementing models that bring together the governance, risk management, and compliance to one platform. These platforms provide:

- Real-time analytics and dashboards
- Continuous control monitoring
- Automated policy enforcement
- Streamlined reporting and audit preparation

Companies minimize fragmentation and enhance the level of transparency in decision-making by the organization through centralization of governance functions.

4. **Governance for Autonomous and Distributed Systems**

   Customers: Governance should embrace the need to include: Systems As systems grow and more autonomous (AI agents, automated workflows, etc.), governance needs to adjust accordingly:

   - Automated control validation
   - Embedded accountability mechanisms
   - Continuous auditability
   - Ethical and operational safeguards

   Regulatory architectures in the future will be required to accommodate systems that operate autonomously but remain transparent, traceable, and compliant with changing legal requirements.

The Direction of Future Regulatory Architecture

The future of governance is never document-driven, but is system-driven. Regulatory imperatives will be more and more codified in platforms, processes and infrastructure. When organizational structures are adjusted to align with governance goals, they will be better positioned to handle complexity, meet new regulations, and retain confidence in highly digitalized settings.

5.2 ENTERPRISE INTEGRATION GOVERNANCE MODELS

Enterprise integration governance refers to how integration standards, policies, security controls, and architectural decisions are governed within an organization. With enterprises using microservices, APIs, cloud solutions, event-based systems, and third-party integrations, integration as a control surface becomes a pivotal point of control that requires a systematic approach to governance.

Without governance, the integration layer will be fragmented. The API is constructed haphazardly. Data flows are undocumented. There are varying security policies in systems. This over time generates architectural sprawl, operational risk, exposure to compliance and technical debt. Governance models provide the framework to ensure consistency, accountability, and traceability across interconnected systems.

Contemporary enterprise integration governance does not depend on documentation or approval processes. It consists of the standardization of policies, architectural reviews, API life cycle management, enforced security, data pedigree tracing, and ongoing integrations monitoring. The control and agility of governance should be balanced to enable innovation without compromising reliability or compliance.

Effective governance models stipulate the decision-makers for integration, enforcement of standards, review of changes, and validation of adherence. They define ownership between platform teams, domain teams, security teams, as well as enterprise architects. Integration governance serves as the foundation for large-scale digital ecosystems, enabling systems to develop smoothly and in a coordinated way, rather than in an anarchic manner.

5.2.1 Centralized vs Federated Integration Governance

1. **Centralized Integration Governance Model**

   A central governance office or committee is set up to supervise and administer all integration-related operations in a centralized integration governance model. Representatives from a variety of departments, including IT, legal, compliance, and business units, may make up this central team. The group is responsible for creating and implementing integration governance guidelines, standards, and practices applicable to the entire company.

   Key characteristics include:

   - Single governance office or Chief Architect controls all decisions
   - Uniform policies enforced enterprise-wide without exceptions
   - Top-down communication of standards and requirements

- Centralized monitoring of compliance, API standards, integration patterns, and quality metrics

Benefits of a centralized governance model

- **Consistency**: Integrity, quality, and uniformity across APIs, services, and data flows are ensured by a centralized approach that applies integration governance principles and standards uniformly throughout the business.
- **Control:** The central governance team can enforce policies, maintain compliance, and protect system security together with privacy protection because they possess complete authority over integration management processes.
- **Compliance:** The centralized governance system helps organizations to meet industry standards and legal requirements because it establishes all policies and procedures from one central authority.

Challenges of a centralized governance model

- **Bottlenecks:** Centralized decision-making creates bottlenecks which reduce operational agility and organizational responsiveness while their integration work experiences delays.
- **Lack of flexibility**: The organization needs flexible solutions because different departments and business units require unique integration methods based their specific needs.
- **Resistance to change**: The departments and individuals who currently use their existing integration processes will resist the implementation of centralized organization-wide policies and standards.

2. **Federated Integration Governance Model**

The company establishes a central governing body to manage integration governance which will operate through its federated integration governance framework. This central authority must create fundamental integration governance standards, which include principles, established practices, and specific recommendations. The various business units within the corporation hold responsibility for implementing and maintaining these established guidelines.

Each business unit or domain establishes its own governance team or committee to oversee integration governance operations. The local teams work with the central governing body to maintain consistency in governance while addressing their specific integration requirements and needs.

Key characteristics include:

- Central council defines high-level policies and standards
- Business units implement guidelines within their domains
- Coordination mechanisms ensure alignment across teams
- Shared accountability between central and domain governance

Benefits of a federated governance model

- **Balance of Control and Flexibility:** A balance between decentralized flexibility and centralized control is offered by the federated approach. The system enables the organization to implement consistent integration governance processes across all departments while allowing each business unit to select its operational procedures based on its unique requirements.
- **Scalability:** The federated model can scale more successfully than a strictly centralized approach as organisations expand and become more complicated. The system achieves higher operational efficiency because its workload and decision-authority distribution across various teams reduces the risk of bottlenecks and enables faster responses to changing business demands.
- **Domain Expertise:** The federated approach enables us to work with subject matter experts from every business unit through our partnership with local teams who possess specific knowledge of their fields. The integration governance procedures require customization because different domains have unique needs and specific requirements.

Challenges of a federated governance model

- **Complexity:** It can be difficult and complex to coordinate and synchronize several governance teams within the organization. A federated model's successful implementation depends on clear lines of communication, well-defined roles and duties, and efficient collaboration systems.
- **Consistency and Standardization:** It might be challenging to guarantee uniform integration governance procedures and standards across all business units, even though the federated model seeks to achieve equilibrium. Maintaining alignment requires strong governance procedures and frequent communication between the central body and local teams.

5.2.2 API Governance and Lifecycle Management

The structure and collection of procedures known as API governance ensure that your APIs are of the highest caliber, consistent, compliant, and aligned with business objectives. Governance includes business-level metadata to facilitate API discovery and consumption, security and API-gateway policy enforcement, and design-style standards and best practices for API coding.

In reality, we frequently observe businesses utilizing an API governance model that includes subsets of rules for various API protocols, patterns, and use cases, as well as a wide range of rules, standards, and policies.

Another essential element of sound API governance is API reporting. Tracking the key performance indicators (KPIs) of your governance initiatives and comprehending the governance maturity of your entire API portfolio are essential.

Essentially, API governance is an essential part of a well-developed API management program and offers the safeguards that lead to excellent APIs.

To put it simply, any organization adopting an API First strategy—where APIs are essential to transformation and regarded as significant business assets—must prioritize API governance.

The proper implementation of API governance is crucial for a certain use case. That's big businesses. You probably already work with hundreds to thousands of various kinds and categories of APIs. With sound governance, these APIs expose your IT and business capabilities and provide a portfolio of API building blocks ready for internal, partner, and customer users to adopt and reuse.

Understanding API Lifecycle Management

API lifecycle management enables organizations to manage their APIs from creation through end-of-life. The structured lifecycle management system provides organizations with essential advantages by treating APIs as operational assets rather than merely technical elements. This method strengthens security measures while ensuring compliance with industry standards through its data protection measures.

Development teams achieve higher productivity because they use standardized processes which eliminate duplicate work to deliver new projects faster. The APIs that result from this process establish trustworthy connections which link essential systems together.

The process of strategic management helps organizations to create better API systems which achieve business goals while enabling their systems to grow through improved integration capabilities. The API lifecycle consists of separate stages which need dedicated resources and best practice methods to achieve successful results.

Organizations that approach API management methodically through these stages can avoid costly failures and unlock opportunities at each phase. The process starts with conception and continues through planning, development, and deployment until it reaches the final stage of retirement which creates a complete framework.

5.2.3 Data Governance in Integrated Ecosystems

Data governance establishes the fundamental operational framework which determines all aspects of data management including its control mechanisms and access rights and protection measures and usage policies throughout the organization. The system provides policies and standards together with ownership models and accountability structures which maintain data integrity and security and accessibility and reliability.

Most organizations face difficulties because they believe governance exists only as documentation which includes a collection of rules that organizations store in Confluence or SharePoint. The actual operation of governance functions as a dynamic system which affects all phases of data management from beginning to end.

A robust data governance program typically includes:

- **Policies:** The organization needs to establish clear guidelines which define acceptable data usage data retention periods security requirements access control models and quality expectations.
- **Standards:** The established rules determine the proper methods for naming data and tagging it and classifying it and structuring it and integrating it and validating it and storing it. Standards reduce inconsistency, duplication, and ambiguity across systems.
- **Data Stewardship:** The organization establishes role-based responsibilities which guarantee data accuracy and track workflows and data lineage and data usage compliance. Data stewards enforce quality checks and serve as custodians for business-critical datasets.
- **Data Ownership:** The system requires clear identification of data ownership to establish responsibility for data management. Data ownership enables people to take responsibility for maintaining data accuracy, controlling access rights, and making decisions about data management.

The integrated environment requires governance to manage data that moves through APIs and cloud platforms and microservices and partner systems while achieving consistent operation and traceable data and regulatory compliance across its interconnected systems.

5.2.4 Integration Policy Enforcement and Architectural Oversight

The organization implements its integration standards and security controls and architectural decisions through its security framework which requires ongoing enforcement across all company operations. The documentation of governance in extensive digital ecosystems that operate through APIs and messaging systems and cloud services and third-party platforms needs to shift from its current state to active enforcement.

Policy Enforcement

The system authenticates requirements through automatic enforcement which it applies to the design, development and operational phases of the process. The contemporary enterprises now use governance as their primary method which they integrate into their operational procedures instead of conducting manual reviews.

Policy enforcement typically includes:

- **Design-Time Controls:** Validation of API specifications, schema definitions, naming conventions, security requirements before development should be proceeded.
- **Build-Time Validation:** The system conducts automated checks during CI/CD pipeline operations to verify that all integrations meet established patterns and security requirements and versioning rules.
- **Runtime Enforcement:** The system implemented API gateway policies which controlled access to resources and enforced rate limits while requiring encryption and monitoring rules during its operational activities.
- **Policy-as-Code Approaches:** Machine-readable formats encoding governance rules ensure consistent and fully automatic enforcement pan-environment.

The organized execution of policies enables organizations to decrease both configuration drift and security vulnerabilities together with their non-compliant integrations.

Architectural Oversight

The architectural control functions as a control mechanism which ensures that integration implementations follow both enterprise architectural standards and business strategies and regulatory requirements. The system establishes architectural governance to manage system relationships and communication methods and development processes which occur over time.

Architectural oversight typically involves:

- **Enterprise Architecture Review Boards:** The enterprise architecture review boards conduct official assessment procedures which evaluate integration designs to establish their compliance with enterprise standards.
- **Approved Integration Patterns**: The approved integration patterns categorize as API design patterns, event-based communication patterns, data interchange patterns, and hybrid cloud integration patterns.
- **Interoperability Standards:** The standards define rules which establish data format requirements, schema specifications, protocol definitions, and metadata standards needed for effective communication between different systems.
- **Lifecycle Alignment:** The process oversees integration assets through two main activities which include version control and the implementation of deprecation methods and the establishment of assets for future use.
- **Compliance and Risk Validation**: The process of validating integrations ensures that they follow all applicable regulatory standards and privacy laws and security requirements that exist in different regions.

The Combined Impact

The system operates through active governance because it requires both policy enforcement and architectural oversight to function. The established integration procedures demonstrate full implementation, which shows their actual functionality. Organizations make architectural decisions based on their business strategies and the need to meet fundamental regulatory requirements.

The two-layer governance system of this organization decreases system fragmentation while improving security and compliance. The system development work for the organization supports its long-term resilience by creating integrated systems, but it also introduces uncontrolled complexity.

5.3 PLATFORM METRICS, FINOPS AND COST OPTIMIZATION

The rising need for cloud native systems together with micro services design and distributed systems has made operational financial responsibility and transparent business practices essential. Platform engineering now requires assessment of economic efficiency because its focus has expanded beyond system reliability and developer productivity to include this new requirement. Organizations learn about system performance through technical assessment and they gain insights into its financial aspects.

All platform metrics become accessible to users which enables them to assess system performance and operational effectiveness and business performance results. The metrics extend beyond standard infrastructure monitoring to measure deployment frequency and change failure rate and resource utilization and cost per workload and value delivery. The combination of engineering metrics with financial expertise allows enterprises to align their technology decisions with their strategic business objectives.

FinOps (Financial Operations) is a discipline that has brought together engineering, finance, and operations teams to manage and optimize cloud expenses. It also fosters a collective responsibility for cost efficiency and ensures that cloud consumption aligns with budgetary and business objectives. FinOps changes the cost management process from periodic reporting to continuous optimization.

Modern platforms require awareness of architecture, transparency in use, and policy-based governance to optimize costs. It consists of the workload right-sizing, automated scaling, resource lifecycle, waste reduction, and cost allocation models. Once platform metrics and FinOps are used jointly, organizations can strike the right balance between the speed of innovation and financial discipline.

5.3.1 Platform Performance and Engineering Metrics

Platform performance and engineering metrics can be useful metrics that allow organizations to determine the effectiveness of their platform engineering initiatives to deliver in terms of speed, reliability, and business value. These metrics go beyond the conventional infrastructure monitoring, as they assess the effectiveness with which teams develop, implement, run and scale digital infrastructure. Structured engineering indicators enable organizations to identify software delivery lifecycle bottlenecks and inefficiencies, as well as potential areas for improvement.

Modern platform teams use research-based performance metrics to assess their software delivery speed and stability through the DORA metrics system.

Core Delivery and Reliability Metrics

- **Deployment Frequency:** The system calculates success rate for code deployments which complete their production process. The organization has achieved its highest level of development because its deployment operations run automatically while its delivery process maintains efficiency and accuracy.
- **Lead Time for Changes:** The code change process requires this duration to move from commit stage to production deployment. The development process performs best when lead times are short, as this enables smoother integration with existing systems.
- **Change Failure Rate:** The percentage shows which deployments need remediation because of their failures. The organization demonstrates improved testing methods through decreased failure rates which show their architectural system operates consistently.
- **Mean Time to Recovery (MTTR):** The speed of team recovery from production failures serves as the measurement for their recovery capacity. Systems with reduced recovery time demonstrate their strength through effective incident management processes.

The combination of these metrics provides complete assessment of engineering efficiency through its assessment of deployment velocity which includes deployment frequency and lead time together with its assessment of system stability which includes change failure rate and MTTR.

Platform-Specific Performance Indicators

Synthetically trained data were used to generate hundreds of models on deep learning networks.

- **Platform Adoption Metrics:** The system tracks the frequency with which developers access internal platform tools and self-service portals and deployment pipelines and shared infrastructure services.
- **Self-Service Utilization:** It is a trial for developers to perform tasks by themselves without the intervention of operations or infrastructure facilities.
- **Onboarding Time:** It assesses how fast new engineer hires can start making a meaningful contribution through the platform.
- **Resource Utilization Metrics:** It keeps track of CPU, RAM, storage, and network usage in order to make sure that the provisioned resources are being utilized efficiently and overprovisioning is minimized.
- **Reliability and Availability Indicators:** It contains uptime percentages, error rates, and service-level indicators (SLIs) as indicators to gauge platform stability.

Connecting Metrics to Business Value

Platform metrices are most effective when linked with business results. The platform should:

- Faster time to market
- Reduced operational risk
- Improved developer productivity
- Lower incident frequency

- Better infrastructure utilization

By continuously measuring engineering performance, organizations create a feedback loop that supports continuous improvement. The financial operations of the organization and its cost reduction efforts use platform metrics as their core metrics to guarantee operational efficiency develops alongside financial performance tracking.

5.3.2 FINOPS Principles and Cloud Financial Governance

Financial Operations (FinOps) was created as an answer to cloud expenses which are unpredictable in the pay-as-you-go model. With the movement of organizations to the public cloud systems, like AWS, Azure, and Google Cloud, during the early 2010s, the old methods of IT cost management were not applicable any longer. New ways of tracking, allocating, forecasting and optimizing costs in real time were needed by variable consumption models.

This change over time came to be organized into a discipline that is now called FinOps - a combination of Finance and DevOps. The FinOps Foundation states that FinOps is a model of operations and culture, the maximum business value of cloud investments, which allows the engineering, finance, and business units to collaborate to make decisions promptly based on the data at hand and ensure financial accountability.

Finops is not just an initiative that aims at cost-cutting. It is a governance model that ensures that cloud consumption is in line with strategic business goals and still remains agile and innovative.

Core Principles of FinOps

FinOps Foundation outlines a list of principles that govern the current cloud financial governance.

- **Cross-Functional Collaboration:** Cloud spending decisions are made by engineering, finance, operations and business teams. This removes silos, as well as, makes the financial consideration integrated into architectural and operational decisions.
- **Business Value–Driven Decisions:** The decisions made by the Cloud spending are measured on the basis of the business value provided. Cost is taken into consideration as well as performance,

reliability, scalability, and revenue impact. The reason behind making certain investments is explained by the quantifiable result rather than by the budgetary limitations in their entirety.

- **Decentralized Accountability with Central Governance:** Teams in this case have the responsibility of their cloud usage and costs. Meanwhile, a centralized FinOps role sets standards, models of allocations, prediction structures, and practices of vendors to provide consistency and controls.
- **Timely and Accessible Financial Data:** The system provides instant operational data together with cost information which helps users make better decisions. The organization uses quick feedback mechanisms to help its teams manage resources while they identify system faults and improve their budgeting predictions.
- **Leveraging the Variable Cost Model:** The company considers its cloud service pricing model which changes according to usage patterns as a competitive strength. Organizations use dynamic resource adjustments to control their consumption patterns while they optimize their spending through dedicated resource commitments.

Cloud Financial Governance Practices

Effective FinOps implementation includes structured governance mechanisms that operationalize these principles:

- Organizations use cost allocation models which include chargeback or show back systems to distribute their expenses across departments and products and services.
- Tagging standards to ensure accurate cost visibility and reporting
- Budget thresholds and automated alerts to detect anomalies
- Continuous resource optimization through right-sizing and elimination of idle assets
- Forecasting and variance analysis to support executive decision-making

- Cross-functional review cycles to evaluate trends and improvement opportunities

These practices transform cloud spending from a reactive financial report into a managed operational capability.

Strategic Benefits of FinOps

FinOps' ability to generate missions creates quantifiable enterprise value:

- Improved cost transparency and predictability
- Stronger alignment between engineering and financial strategy
- Reduced waste and optimized resource utilization
- Faster, data-driven decision-making
- Enhanced accountability across teams
- Scalable financial governance as cloud adoption grows

Finally, FinOps implants engineering in-platform engineering with financial intelligence. By combining measures, control, and price responsibility, organizations can be sure that cloud investment helps them move forward with innovation, restore, and develop continuously.

5.3.3 Cost Optimization Strategies in Modern Architectures

Once organizations establish cost visibility and the appropriate governance structure, targeted optimization strategies can drastically cut cloud expenditures. A hybrid approach frequently yields better results than trying to optimise everything within a single cloud provider, because different workloads have different cost profiles. Businesses cut expenses without sacrificing performance through the following strategies.

1. **Rightsize Compute and Storage**

   The majority of workloads use instances that are bigger than they need to be. Aligning instance types with real resource usage is known as rightsizing. An application is probably overprovisioned if it routinely consumes less than 20% of the CPU and memory that are available. Without compromising performance, compute costs can be lowered by 30–50% by downsizing instances or moving to more efficient instance families.

In order to identify realistic usage patterns, the first step in effective rightsizing is to analyse CPU, memory, disc, and network utilisation for a minimum of two weeks. Strong candidates for downsizing are those that routinely operate at or below 40% utilisation. It is common for newer instance generations to offer better performance at a cheaper cost.

For sustained high-utilization workloads, enterprise analysis may reveal that certain systems are more cost-efficient in private cloud or colocation environments than in public cloud, particularly when long-term consumption patterns are considered.

2. **Shut Down Idle and Unused Resources**

   Seldom do development and staging environments need to run continuously. For those workloads, scheduling non-production resources to shut down during off-peak hours can reduce expenditures by 65–75%. Implementation is made easier with automated scheduling technologies.

   The same holds true for resources that are forgotten or underutilised, such out-of-date test instances, detached storage volumes, and out-of-date snapshots. Frequent cycles of clean-up avoid unnecessary cost accumulation.

3. **Use Reserved Instances, Savings Plans, and Spot Capacity**

   Committed-use discounts offer significant savings for steady and predictable workloads. Compared to on-demand pricing, compute expenses can be lowered by 30–70% with reserved instances and savings plans. For fault-tolerant batch systems, spot or preemptible instances work well workloads and can offer discounts of up to 90%.

   Committed pricing, however, creates financial danger for the business. The company faces two problems because of its commitment. Organizations must carefully align commitment levels with realistic usage forecasts. Hybrid strategies enable organizations to increase their operational capacity through a system that combines fixed base capacity with flexible infrastructure components.

4. **Autoscaling and Dynamic Scaling Policies**

   The practice of maintaining all-time peak load capacity results in excessive operational costs. The autoscaling system enables automatic resource capacity adjustments which match current user demand by increasing resources during peak times and decreasing them during off-peak hours.

   The development of effective scaling rules enables organizations to achieve 40 to 60 percent cost savings while maintaining their operational performance and system availability according to their needs.

5. **Optimize Data Egress and Network Costs**

   The total cloud computing expenses of an organization face significant influence from data transfer charges which include egress fees as a major component. The essential methods for controlling expenses need organizations to reduce cross-border data movement and optimize their content delivery networks and assess their data transmission patterns.

   Dedicated connectivity solutions provide hybrid architectures with reduced transfer expenses and enhanced operational efficiency. The system needs to design its architecture to handle work processes which send out large amounts of data while minimizing unnecessary data transmission.

6. **Implement Tiered Storage and Lifecycle Policies**

   Not every piece of data needs expensive storage. Storage expenses can be reduced by 80 to 90 percent through the process of moving infrequently accessed data to more economical storage solutions or to preservation storage. The system transfers data between storage levels through its automated lifecycle controls, which operate based on access patterns to achieve efficient results without requiring human control.

7. **Leverage Serverless, Containers, and Managed Services**

   Organizations pay for their actual computing needs instead of paying for unused resources through computing power operationalized through serverless systems and container-based systems. Managed services provide a solution which reduces infrastructure management expenses.

   The services have higher costs per unit but they provide better value through increased resource usage and simpler operational management.

8. **Use Cost Anomaly Detection and Alerting**

   The automated anomaly detection systems identify sudden increases in spending that were not anticipated before those issues reached their critical point. The system provides immediate alerts which enable teams to respond to configuration problems and security breaches and unexpected usage increases thus avoiding unplanned expenses.

   Modern architectural systems require ongoing cost optimization efforts as their essential operation which continues throughout the lifecycle. Organizations can achieve performance and scalability and financial responsibility through these methods when they combine FinOps governance with platform performance metrics as their foundation for maximizing cloud investments.

5.4 AI-ASSISTED INTEGRATION AND INTELLIGENT AUTOMATION

Enterprise systems are more distributed, event-centric and data-driven. Organizations are active in a hybrid cloud platform, SaaS digital environment, edge infrastructure, and microservices interconnectivity. With increasing complexity of the system, the conventional rule-based integration patterns and fixed automation paradigms are not able to retain agility, scale, and resilience. Modern architectures need intelligence to be incorporated on the integration and orchestration layers directly.

The integration with the help of AI adds Predictive analytics, natural language processing, and machine learning to middleware and enterprise connectivity platforms. Instead of using fixed mappings and fixed workflows, systems are able to analyze patterns, learn through past behavior and dynamically adjust the logic of integration. This will be a shift towards deterministic orchestration to context-sensitive, adaptive integration.

This concept goes further than connectivity to intelligent automation. It uses AI-based decision-making to business processes, infrastructure management, incident responses, and operational processes. Automation is no longer seen as a way to perform a predetermined course of action, rather it is able to check conditions, anticipate results and facilitate optimized responses on the fly.

Event streams, autonomous services, and APIs are becoming structurally available under enterprise architecture as organizations grow digital ecosystems and become more dependent on them. With the integration of intelligence into integration layers and automation layers, businesses are able to increase their efficiency, lower the operational risk, and build systems that can be constantly optimized.

5.4.1 AI in Enterprise Integration Platforms

AI-powered integration refers to the use of artificial intelligence to automate and enhance the integration of systems, applications, and data sources that organizations rely on daily.

The implementation of AI-powered integration varies depending on complexity and use case requirements. In some scenarios, AI assists in building low-code connectors for newly adopted systems. The system automatically creates custom scripts which run complex synchronization processes between various enterprise platforms. The system connects IT service management systems with CRM tools and DevOps platforms and customer support applications.

The traditional integration methods need both custom coding work and manual setup work and continuous system upkeep work. AI uses its advanced analytical capabilities together with its natural language processing functions and its machine learning algorithms to transform the process through three main components which include data mapping and workflow automation and human error reduction.

- **AI-Powered Integration Capabilities**

  AI Support Frameworks present capability of intelligence properties, which we translate as reliability, scalability, and efficiency.

- **Smart Data Mapping**

  Data mapping stands as the most challenging element of integration work. AI uses schemas and metadata together with historical usage data to create automatic field mappings between different systems. The system can identify semantic connections between different platforms because it understands vocabulary differences.

  AI systems can match fields between different systems by understanding that a "Customer Account" field in one system is equivalent to a "Company" field in another system. The system proves useful for organizations that must connect multiple systems which contain various customized fields.

- **Intelligent Error Detection and Correction**

  All large-scale integrations face the problem of data inconsistencies which they need to resolve. The AI models perform three functions because they detect anomalies and they identify failure patterns and they produce remediation recommendations. AI-powered systems identify root causes of errors which include data type mismatches and missing required fields and API rate limit violations. The system enables automatic application of corrective actions which leads to better integration stability and lower operational costs.

- **AI-Driven Business Process Automation**

  AI improves integration platforms through its ability to create adaptable workflow changes which use current data. Operational settings including supply chain management and service management and customer operations use integration workflows that can automatically modify themselves to meet new conditions.

Organizations achieve higher operational efficiency through machine learning model integration and automated processes that run through their entire system.

- **Predictive Insights**

  AI systems use historical synchronization data and system behavior patterns to predict future system disruptions. The predictive models help to detect two main patterns which include recurring performance bottlenecks and seasonal traffic spikes.

  AI uses historical data synchronization patterns which show that quarterly end periods experience increased volume to automatically modify synchronization times and to notify system administrators about upcoming problems. The system uses predictive capabilities to improve its operational durability and system dependability.

- **Natural Language Processing for Configuration**

  Natural language processing makes it easier to perform complex system integrations because it enables users to express their integration needs through normal language, which the AI system uses to create configuration rules based on the abilities of connected systems. The method allows organizations to execute projects more quickly while their technical departments maintain the power to assess and enhance all created work.

  Organizations use AI-driven integration solutions throughout their contemporary business operations. Organizations achieve dynamic, intelligent integration systems through the implementation of intelligence within their middleware and orchestration components, which results in continuous system development and improvement.

5.4.2 Intelligent Automation in DevOps and Platform Engineering

The practice called intelligent automation in DevOps and platform engineering uses artificial intelligence together with machine learning to enhance and optimize all tasks which occur during the software delivery lifecycle. The standard DevOps automation system requires users to execute predefined scripts together with established pipelines and system operations. In the present day of AI usage, automation has shifted from executing fixed rules to creating systems which can learn from past experiences and use pattern recognition to make decisions based on their surrounding environment.

AI powered automation in DevOps processes uses telemetry data and log files and build results and deployment measurements and production metrics to identify operational weaknesses and forecast potential system breakdowns. Intelligent systems possess the capability to monitor build pipelines for abnormal activity and they can forecast deployment disruptions while providing recommendations to minimize user impact before disruptions happen. The teams can now transform their practice of solving problems through active fault-finding into a method of preventing system errors through reliability management.

Intelligent automation in platform engineering improves operational capacity through its ability to manage infrastructure and deliver services. AI models optimize CI/CD processes by identifying pipeline changes and detecting configuration drift, and automatically creating environments based on usage patterns. The AI system conducts continuous system analysis which helps maintain platform system integrity while decreasing platform operational expenses.

The field of intelligent automation has achieved its most important development through the creation of predictive analytics. Machine learning algorithms use past deployment information and failure rates and show performance trends to predict instability or a bottleneck. The system will detect high-risk situations through its ability to monitor specific deployment patterns which result in rollback events before it starts the execution process. AI-based scaling systems use their workload-spiking prediction to adjust infrastructure capacity through automated control mechanisms.

DevOps productivity is also increased through natural language interfaces and AI assistants. Conversational prompts can help engineers query state of the system, request deployment insights, or get a summary of incidents, so that they do not need to analyze logs manually. This enhances the availability of operational intelligence as well as governance controls.

Organizations deploy AI into DevOps pipelines and platform engineering workflows to accelerate the deployment speed, enhance the reliability, and minimize the human error. Smart automation turns the delivery pipelines into dynamic systems that can constantly learn and optimize and help scale and resiliate enterprise architecture.

5.4.3 AIOps and Autonomous Infrastructure Management

The use of "artificial intelligence" (AI) capabilities, such as machine learning models and natural language processing, to automate, optimize, and streamline IT service management and operational workflows is known as artificial intelligence for IT operations, or AIOps.

AIOps leverages big data, analytics and ML capabilities to:

- In a corporate tech stack, ingest and aggregate the massive (and constantly growing) amounts of data produced by IT components, application needs, performance monitoring tools, and service ticketing systems.
- To find important events and trends pertaining to application performance and availability problems, intelligently separate signals from the "noise."
- Determine the underlying causes of problems and report them to IT and DevOps for prompt incident response and remediation; occasionally, these problems can be automatically resolved without the need for human interaction.

With end-to-end insight and context, AIOps allows IT operations teams to react swiftly—and frequently proactively—to outages and slowdowns by combining disparate manual IT operations technologies into a single intelligent, automated IT operations (ITOps) platform.

It assists companies in bridging the gap between user expectations of app availability and performance and diverse, dynamic, and challenging-to-monitor IT landscapes and siloed IT teams. AIOps is viewed by many experts as the future of IT operations management due to the widespread adoption of digital transformation projects across business sectors.

AIOps Components

AIOps can use a variety of AI techniques and functionalities, including as algorithms, data aggregation, machine learning, analytics, automation and visualization.

Algorithms allow AIOps platforms to prioritize events and make performance decisions by codifying IT expertise, business logic, and goals. Machine learning is based on algorithms, which allow platforms to set baselines and adjust when environmental data changes.

To assist systems, learn from big datasets and adjust to new knowledge, machine learning employs strategies like supervised, unsupervised, reinforcement, and deep learning. Anomaly detection, root cause analysis (RCA), event correlation, and predictive analysis are all supported by machine learning in AIOps.

In order to produce new data and metadata that assist teams and systems in identifying patterns, isolating issues, forecasting capacity requirements, and managing events, analytics analyze raw operational data.

AIOps systems can respond to real-time insights thanks to automation features. Predictive analytics, for instance, could foresee a spike in traffic and initiate an automated process to distribute more resources according to predefined rules.

Data Visualization presents insights utilizing graphical user interfaces, statistics, and dashboards to enable IT teams to track developments and make defensible choices beyond automated responses.

Working of AIOps

AIOps unifies disparate ITOps teams, tools, and data into a single system by utilizing a big data platform. This information could consist of:

- Historical performance and event data
- Real-time operational events
- System logs and metrics
- Network and infrastructure data
- Incident and ticketing data
- Application demand data

Analytics and machine learning tools are used by AIOps platforms to:

- Keep important warnings apart from background noise by identifying abnormal patterns.
- Correlate events across environments to identify root causes and propose solutions.
- Automate responses, including proactive and real-time remediation.
- Learn continuously and adapt to environmental changes such as new infrastructure provisioning or configuration updates.

Implementing AIOps

The journey to AIOps differs across organizations, but it typically begins with integrating tools that improve visibility, predictive capabilities and automated response.

Key capabilities include:

- **Observability**

  Observability allows teams to comprehend complex systems' underlying states based on external outputs. Greater observability enables faster and more accurate movement from performance symptoms to root causes.

- **Predictive Analytics**

  Statistical modelling, machine learning, and historical data are used in predictive analytics to find trends and forecast potential system events. In AIOps, this enables proactive risk detection and capacity planning.

- **Proactive Response and Incident Automation**

Some AIOps solutions automatically respond to unexpected events which include system outages and performance slowdowns. The system predicts future problems by using performance metrics which enter predictive models and start automatic problem resolution. The implementation of incident response automation improves "mean time to detection" (MTTD) metrics while decreasing the need for human monitoring.

5.4.4 Generative AI and Developer Productivity in Integration Workflows

The Generative AI systems use advanced models that create new content by analyzing data patterns which they have learned from their training material. The integration of generative AI technology enables organizations to transition their automated processes from fixed Scripting methods to intelligent systems which can make decisions and change their behavior during ongoing operations.

The generative AI system has the ability to handle unstructured data which includes emails and documents as well as API specifications and tickets and logs to generate custom responses. The ability to generate AI solutions makes them suitable for handling work processes which involve changing system interfaces and unpredictable work patterns. Organizations that implement generative AI into their development platforms gain access to automated workflows which help developers work more efficiently by transforming data and requirements into usable results.

The effectiveness of traditional automation systems is restricted by their dependence on established rules. The introduction of generative AI creates a new system which enables AI agents to perform independent tasks through agentic workflows. Generative AI enables support throughout the entire integration process because it helps with trigger detection and schema interpretation and mapping generation and execution.

Key phases in this shift include:

- **From Reactive to Proactive:** Generated AI examines the patterns of integrational logs and system behavior to predict any problem that is about to arise whenever possible.
- **Multimodal Integration:** A generative AI helps to weave text, structured data, and event streams together to generate/integrate logical integration aspects and refine them.
- **Continuous Learning:** Digitally scrawled scripts in an AI format can often seem a bit complex for constant value, considering this quality is not easy.

We believe with generative AI incorporated into integration platforms and developer environments; enterprise systems could be streamlined significantly.

Core Elements in Generative AI–Driven Integration

Possible elements of AI–generated workflow modules include:

- **Triggers and Inputs**: Workflows activate through API calls, scheduled jobs, webhooks, or incoming data streams, while generative AI interprets these inputs to produce executable logic through its translation of requirements.
- **Context Building and Reasoning**: Through retrieval-augmented generation methods, generative AI uses enterprise knowledge together with documentation and schema context to create outputs that comply with specific business rules. The reasoning layer handles two tasks because it needs to assess multiple options while it creates integration plans and directs task assignments.
- **Execution and Feedback**: The system uses APIs and workflow engines to execute its generated logical operations. The feedback system enables continuous improvement which results in workflows that become more precise and dependable over time.
- **Human Oversight**: The process of human-in-the-loop validation provides a system that guarantees compliance with governance requirements while protecting architectural integrity and enabling traceability.

Enhancing Developer Productivity

Machine learning is said to be the next big thing; specialist responsible for explaining machine-learning projects and their results to the technical illiterates must be fluent in the language spoken while coding.

- **AI-Assisted Code Generation**: The developers use natural language to explain their system integration needs which enables them to obtain generated API calls and transformation scripts and workflow templates that eliminate the need for repetitive code writing.
- **Intelligent Data Mapping**: Generative AI supports automatic field mapping suggestion and generation by analyzing schemas across systems, thus minimizing the necessity for manual configuration.
- **Automated Documentation and Contextual Support**: The developers gained better understanding of unfamiliar APIs through the combination of AI-generated explanations and inline assistance which reduced their need to switch between different work contexts.
- **Error Detection and Optimization**: Generative AI, by its analysis of logs and failures, can make suggestions that make the debugging cycle less long.

Developers can now dedicate their time to architectural design work and optimization processes and innovation tasks because generative AI automates repetitive integration work.

5.5 FUTURE TRENDS IN ENTERPRISE INTEGRATION AND PLATFORMS

Cloud-native designs and AI-inspired automation and decentralized control and hyperconnected ecosystems create new possibilities for enterprises to integrate their platform engineering operations. Organizations are transitioning from traditional ESB-based integration systems which use tightly integrated models to modern integration systems that rely on distributed event-driven API-first platform-based architectures.

The current digital transformation efforts of organizations require more than system connections to achieve integration. The development of operations has evolved into a strategic capability which supports agile operations while driving innovation and creating market advantages. The platforms now develop autonomous environments through their intelligent systems yet they transform their fundamental systems to support governance, observability, cost optimization, and AI-based decision-making systems.

The contemporary cloud computing systems establish multi-cloud and hybrid cloud and edge computing and Software as a Service ecosystem as their primary architectural challenge. The next generation enterprise platforms should hence be able to facilitate interoperability in heterogeneous environments at the same time they should be resilient, secure and compliant. The system needs to use composable architectures together with automation-first operational methods and continuous change integration techniques.

In the future, it is possible to expect that enterprise integration will be characterized by smart orchestration, decentralized ownership patterns, policy-as-code implementation, AI-assisted development, and adaptive infrastructure. The trends below depict the way the integration platforms are changing to suit the needs of the next generation digital businesses.

5.5.1 Composable and API-First Architecture

A contemporary method for creating digital applications is called "composable architecture," which assembles necessary system capabilities from modular, API-based components rather than supplying them all at once.

By adding or changing specific components, this method enables businesses to automate digital activities, connect disparate content repositories, and offer new business capabilities without completely redesigning the system.

By dissecting the features of comprehensive monolithic suites into discrete microservices, you may incorporate the necessary tools into a system that is adaptable and interconnected. Because of this flexibility and modularity, developers can use strong new capabilities and repurpose existing components for increased efficiency.

Composable architectures are created by connecting these separate microservices via APIs.

Composable architectures enable the utilization of content to power scalable, compelling customer experiences, whether they are orchestrated on another platform or developed on top of Concertful.

Microservices architecture, modular architecture, and best-of-breed architecture are all comparable to this framework.

Additionally, software vendors, systems integrators, organisations, and individual specialists are members of the MACH Alliance, a non-profit advocacy group that is particularly helpful in directing the choice of composable technologies.

An application programming interface (API) is a computer software that acts as an intermediary between two applications to ensure that they communicate comfortably. APIs are as old as contemporary computers exist and have numerous applications.

They can increase productivity and collaboration by integrating software and systems to assist internal workflows and processes at businesses. They can assist businesses in integrating software with their partner to provide clients with enhanced or expanded offerings and experiences. Alternatively, they can be made openly accessible to everyone.

In API-first architecture, designers and developers first create the API specification. During the process:

- You first develop the API to ensure consistency
- Next, developers can reuse the APIs for different projects
- Finally, developers maintain consistency, efficiency and scalability throughout the development process

This approach is quickly becoming a globally accepted development method for enhancing system projects and delivering the best user experience.

Benefits of the API-first architecture

It is evident that the API-first development approach has several benefits when contrasted with conventional development approaches. Among them are the following:

- **Faster time-to-market:** Teams don't have to wait on each other; they can build at the same time. That means features get out the door quicker, and your users see value faster.
- **Better user experience:** Developers may improve user experiences by creating dependable, efficient, and consistent user interfaces with an API contract.
- **Improved developer experience:** Developers love working with well-defined APIs. They have an idea of what to expect, can reuse components and spend less time fixing issues. It allows teams to concentrate on what is truly important.
- **Scalability:** API-first makes it simple to scale your business. It would allow you to add new functions, develop more platforms to use or manage a greater number of people without the need to revamp your entire system. It scales as your business grows.
- **Smooth collaboration:** When everyone operates on the same API contract, it becomes easier to collaborate. Product managers, designers and developers remain on the same page, ensuring fewer surprises and quicker delivery.

5.5.2 Event-Driven and Real-Time Enterprise

A software design paradigm known as "event-driven architecture" (EDA) is based on the publication, recording, processing, and archiving of events.

Teams can use it to recognize system events—basically, any action or change that takes place within the system—and react to them in real time, or almost real time.

The widespread use of EDAs in cloud-native settings signifies a dramatic departure from conventional computational architectures, which concentrate on storing static data in repositories such as data lakes (as in service-oriented architectures), in favour of a dynamic strategy that follows data as it moves through an architecture. In an event-driven system, data is still useful, but EDAs prioritize prompt response to events, acknowledging that an event's value may decrease over time.

Event producers (such as microservices, APIs, and IoT devices) transmit real-time event alerts to event consumers in an event-driven architecture. These consumers subsequently initiate particular processing routines. When Netflix releases a new original series, for example, a number of EDA services wait on standby for the release notification, which sets off a sequence of updates to notify users.

The decoupled relationship between front-end and back-end components, which enables systems to exchange information without knowing one another, is one of the main benefits of an event-driven design. customers can receive events without requesting them from producers, while producers can send events without knowing which customers will receive them. To put it another way, EDAs let systems to function autonomously and handle events asynchronously.

With their extensive digital footprints, modern, forward-thinking firms can respond swiftly to event broadcasts and maintain operational readiness without idling thanks to the real-time capability of an event-driven system. As a result, EDAs assist businesses in automating various organizational procedures, such as supply chain optimization and proactive quality problem identification, which eventually boosts their revenue and profitability.

An organization that functions as a real-time enterprise possesses the ability to detect and analyze business events while delivering immediate responses to these events. The real-time enterprise operates on continuous data streams which enable its digital systems to make instant decisions and execute adaptive responses unlike traditional enterprises that depend on scheduled updates and batch processing.

Enterprises execute their operations by processing real-time operational data which flows through their systems instead of storing it for future analysis. The system enables organizations to identify anomalies while they create workflows and update services because it operates without the need for scheduled data synchronization.

Enterprises use event-driven architecture together with continuous data processing and automated decision-making to transform their response systems into adaptive systems which function at digital speed.

5.5.3 Autonomous and AI-Driven Enterprise Platforms

The introduction of e-commerce together with the development of the internet created fundamental changes that transformed how businesses deliver value to customers and operate their organizational structures. The autonomous enterprise has brought about a fundamental shift in how businesses create and execute their strategic plans. The two types of organizations which test automation technologies through their operations show different results than organizations which fully adopt autonomous systems. The autonomous enterprise system operates most of its processes without human intervention while it uses automation to handle most of its operational duties.

The company achieves its core business functions through AI-based decision systems which operate with minimal human input and through agentic process automation. The system uses APA to control entire business operations through its ability to manage multiple systems which include ERP and CRM and SCM and finance through their complete operational duration. The system uses intelligent AI agents which possess decision-making abilities and autonomous operation skills to achieve its goals.

The AI agents work together without any interruptions to their work because they can access all data and systems and all information from different departments. The system processes incoming data streams which include operational data and market shifts and consumer feedback to determine subsequent actions.

An autonomous enterprise changes the way humans work because it does not eliminate their jobs. Workers shift from performing repetitive tasks to managing AI systems while they develop new business strategies that focus on innovation and strategic business growth.

Core components of an autonomous enterprise

The autonomous organization relies on agentic process automation as its main operational method. The implementation of AI agents for complete process control with minimal human involvement represents a ground-breaking method for managing business operations. The AI agents are designed to execute complex tasks through their ability to move through complex workflows and make independent decisions.

The systems achieve unstructured data processing through the integration of AI capabilities and operational functions which enable them to detect patterns and make decisions based on data analysis.

The APA system provides horizontal integration which differs from traditional automation systems that create vertical point solutions to handle particular departmental tasks. The AI agents create a complete business environment which operates seamlessly between different applications.

The horizontal method creates organizational boundaries which workers cannot detect yet which control their work processes. The horizontal approach redirects organizational elements to achieve better efficiency and productivity while working towards common strategic objectives.

Orchestration serves as the essential component that enables the autonomous enterprise to control its multiple automation systems and AI agents. The process requires the synchronization of various systems and activities to achieve efficient operational collaboration. Through effective orchestration AI agents gain the ability to operate on multiple platforms while eliminating conflicts and redundant elements and optimizing resource usage.

Multiple Choice Questions (MCQs)

1. **What is the primary goal of compliance-driven architecture in enterprise integration?**

   A. Reducing hardware usage

   B. Ensuring systems meet regulatory and legal requirements

   C. Eliminating all manual processes

   D. Increasing marketing performance

2. **Audit-ready architectures help organizations mainly by:**
   A. Avoiding system testing
   B. Simplifying financial transactions
   C. Providing traceability, monitoring, and documentation for audits
   D. Eliminating security policies
3. **Enterprise integration governance primarily focuses on:**
   A. Managing office infrastructure
   B. Defining policies, standards, and responsibilities for integration systems
   C. Increasing product sales
   D. Developing standalone applications
4. **Which component is essential in a strong integration governance model?**
   A. Random system deployment
   B. Standardized policies and architectural guidelines
   C. Removal of data security controls
   D. Disconnected services
5. **What does FinOps mainly address in modern platform engineering?**
   A. Financial operations and cloud cost optimization
   B. Software testing automation
   C. Human resource management
   D. Hardware design
6. **Platform metrics are primarily used to:**
   A. Track performance, reliability, and operational efficiency
   B. Replace integration tools
   C. Eliminate data storage
   D. Reduce system documentation

7. **AI-assisted integration helps organizations by:**
   A. Removing all integration platforms
   B. Automating workflows and improving intelligent decision-making
   C. Eliminating data pipelines
   D. Reducing system monitoring
8. **Intelligent automation in enterprise platforms combines:**
   A. Artificial intelligence with automation technologies
   B. Manual workflows with spreadsheets
   C. Hardware and networking only
   D. Accounting and marketing tools
9. **Which emerging trend is influencing the future of enterprise integration?**
   A. Isolated legacy systems
   B. AI-driven integration platforms and low-code tools
   C. Completely manual data exchange
   D. Reduction of digital services
10. **Future enterprise integration platforms are expected to emphasize:**
   A. Centralized manual processes
   B. Scalability, automation, and AI-driven capabilities
   C. Removal of APIs
   D. Decreased interoperability

Answers

1	2	3	4	5	6	7	8	9	10
B	C	B	B	A	A	B	A	B	B

Bibliography

Adusumilli, T. (2025) 'Enterprise system integration: Foundations, technologies, and strategic impacts in modern business environments', *World Journal of Advanced Engineering Technology and Sciences*, 15(1), pp. 346–356. Available at: https://doi.org/10.30574/wjaets.2025.15.1.0205.

Alawami, A. (2022) 'Evolution of Enterprise Application Integration Technologies', *International Journal of Computer Science and Information Technology Research*, 10(2), pp. 50–54. Available at: https://doi.org/10.5281/zenodo.6536509.

Batra, M. (2025) *GraphQL, Medium*. Available at: https://medium.com/@contactmanoharbatra/graphql-5cf1916f99e7.

GeeksforGeeks (2025a) *API Contracts - System Design*. Available at: https://www.geeksforgeeks.org/system-design/api-contracts-system-design/.

GeeksforGeeks (2025b) *What is RestFul API?* Available at: https://www.geeksforgeeks.org/node-js/what-is-restful-api/.

Gulledge, T.R. (2008) 'Architecture-driven Enterprise Integration', 5(3), pp. 265–309.

Lin, G. and Macvittie, L.A. (2022) *Enterprise Architecture for Digital Business Compliments of.*

Myerson, J.M. (2001) *Enterprise Systems Second Edition.*

Vallejo, C., Romero, D. and Molina, A. (2012) 'Enterprise integration engineering reference framework and toolbox', *International Journal of*

Production Research, 50(6), pp. 1489–1511. Available at: https://doi.org/10.1080/00207543.2011.560200.

Xu, L. Da (2014) *Enterprise Integration and Information Architecture: A Systems Perspective on Industrial Information Integration, 2014 Enterprise Systems Conference.* Available at: http://ieeexplore.ieee.org/lpdocs/epic03/wrapper.htm?arnumber=6997051.

About the Authors

Srikanth Sriramoju is an experienced Enterprise Integration Architect with over a decade of expertise in designing and delivering large-scale integration and digital transformation solutions. He specializes in connecting complex enterprise systems, enabling seamless data flow across customer platforms, financial systems, workforce applications, and operational environments. His core strengths include API-led integration, event-driven architectures, and building scalable, resilient technology ecosystems.

Throughout his career, Srikanth has led high-impact initiatives that modernize legacy infrastructures, streamline business processes, and support real-time, data-driven operations. He combines deep technical proficiency with a strategic architectural mindset, helping organizations build adaptable and future-ready systems.

In addition to his professional work, Srikanth actively contributes to research and knowledge sharing in enterprise integration, distributed systems, and intelligent automation. His work focuses on translating complex concepts into practical solutions that bridge the gap between theory and real-world enterprise implementation.

Prashanth Kodati is a seasoned Cloud DevOps and Platform Engineering leader with deep expertise in building and operating scalable, cloud-native infrastructure across complex enterprise environments. He specializes in designing automation-first platforms that enhance reliability, security, and operational efficiency. With a strong focus on Infrastructure as Code (IaC), CI/CD, and Kubernetes-based delivery systems, he has enabled organizations to modernize legacy systems and accelerate digital transformation.

Throughout his career, Prashanth has led large-scale initiatives spanning multi-cloud architectures, SaaS platforms, cloud migrations, and AI-driven data ecosystems. His experience across Microsoft Azure, AWS, and Google Cloud allows him to architect resilient, high-performance solutions tailored to enterprise needs.

Combining hands-on engineering with strategic platform thinking, he empowers organizations to build adaptable, secure, and future-ready cloud systems that support mission-critical workloads and evolving business demands.

www.ingramcontent.com/pod-product-compliance
Lightning Source LLC
LaVergne TN
LVHW022208200926
848481LV00006B/1894

* 9 7 9 8 9 0 3 9 2 9 3 0 6 *